Karma Buster

Heal Yourself
and Create the Life
You Were Meant to Live

Joe Nunziata

www.karmabuster.com

Library of Congress Cataloging-in-Publication Data

Nunziata, Joe
Karma Buster
ISBN: 9780970161598

Contact us:
5405 Alton Parkway, Suite 395
Irvine, CA 92604
Site: www.jnunziata.com
Site: www.karmabuster.com

Dedication

This book is dedicated to my parents, Anna and Joseph, who passed on their karma giving me the opportunity to have this amazing experience here on earth. I now realize that every day here is a blessing regardless of the external situation or circumstance.

See every moment as a magical step along your unique journey to wholeness.

Table of Contents

Forward vii

Introduction ix

1 The Real Deal with Karma Busting 1

2 Your Karmic Wheel 21

3 Why You Selected Your Parents 29

4 Busting Out of Your Ego-Identity 43

5 Your Good and Bad List 55

6 Your Karmic Map and Chakra Energy System 61

7 Do You Really Have a Destiny? 65

8 Maintaining Your Karma Busting Ways Daily 79

9 Creating Your Life in a Whole New Way 83

10 Allowing Yourself to Receive 91

11 Turning on the Lights 109

Also by Joe Nunziata 113

Forward

This book is going to take you on an amazing journey. It is a journey into healing your soul at a deep, emotional level. If you dare to take the first step, your life will be changed forever. In the process of examining your past and looking at your life from a new perspective, you will be transforming yourself.

You will be going down a new road. Joe and I like to call it "the yellow brick road." And just like Dorothy in the *Wizard of Oz,* it was only when she faced her fears and gathered up the courage, heart and mental attitude to go down the road that she changed her life and was able to go home again.

Our spiritual and emotional journey as human beings is to learn our life lessons and make peace with the past. That is the purpose of our mission here on earth. We can take comfort in knowing that every single experience is perfect for you to uncover the lessons that you are here to learn in this lifetime. In dealing with the repressed emotions of the past, you will be able to heal your soul in this lifetime. Each and every human being is trying to complete their specific mission.

We have come to this earthly plane as a soul housed inside a human body. Our deepest desire is to grow, evolve and heal our souls. We reconnect to our true selves when we remember that we are connected to God and that God is love. It is only when we know ourselves as God that we are able to open up our hearts and offer kindness, compassion and understanding to one another. When we accept that we are all the same in spirit, we are able to look at each other without criticism, judgment or blame. We are all one. We are all the same. We are all the spirit of God that is within us. And when we realize that simple fact, we will be able to not only heal ourselves, but also heal the world around us.

My thoughts and prayers are with you as you take on this amazing challenge. I would like to offer you a few helpful tips before you begin your journey. Please remember:

1. Accept every circumstance as a blessing.
2. Be in your truth about everything that happens.
3. Forgive those who have caused you pain.
4. Be yourself and love yourself every single day.

I wish you great success, with loving kindness from the God spirit within me to the God spirit within you.

Namaste,
Marie Theresa D'Angelo
Recently transformed into:
Maria Nunziata

Introduction

Did you know your karma holds the key to your entire life? Every aspect of life – your relationships, your health, your career, your business and your happiness – are tied to your karmic map. If you want to know why you are doing what you do, or why you seem to be struggling in certain areas of your life, you must look to your karma.

The concept of karma has been around for thousands of years yet every person seems to have a different definition. As I began working on this book, I started to ask every person I saw the same question: "*What is your definition of karma?*"

I was interested in the opinions of people from all walks of life. I asked business people, social workers, artists, teachers, spiritualists and truck drivers. In the end I received a series of viewpoints, with most being quite vague.

Following is a composite of the answers I received to the question "*What is karma?*"

- You reap what you sow.
- Every action comes back to you, good or bad.

- Cause and effect.
- You get what you deserve.
- Some people are lucky and others are not.
- We get what we put out based on our intention.
- What goes around comes around.
- It is your destiny.

I could have written an entire book about the variety of definitions I received pertaining to karma. In addition to my informal poll, I researched other definitions based on religious beliefs and ancient traditions.

The most accepted definition comes from Hinduism and Buddhism. It states: *the total effect of a person's actions and conduct during the successive phases of the person's existence, regarded as determining the person's destiny.*

This definition sounds a lot like cause and effect.

Then there are Christian religious writings, or Theosophy, which incorporate beliefs from Buddhism and Brahmanism. Their definition of karma is the *doctrine of inevitable consequence or predetermined destiny.* They define karma as the belief that your entire life is mapped out and there is nothing you can do about it.

I studied these philosophies and then went on my own quest for an answer to the question. After much research, meditation and work with enlightened masters, I have developed a deeper meaning and understanding of karma.

This life-changing book is going to demystify karma and show you how karma effects every minute of your life. You will also gain a much greater knowledge of your specific karma and why you chose it. As you begin to see and understand your karma in a whole new way, I will give you the tools to become a karma buster and change the direction of your life.

You will be introduced to many concepts and processes that can be used on a daily basis to elevate your awareness and help you make changes "that stick." This is an ongoing process and you will become more and more proficient at it as you gain awareness and experience.

All I ask is that you remain open to new ideas and philosophies about karma and your life. My goal is to empower you with tools to help you create the life you were meant to live.

1 The Real Deal with Karma Busting

Let's start with a new definition of karma. Before I do, let me tell you how I ventured onto this path. I never imagined that I would write a book like this one.

I was born in a lower middle class section of Brooklyn, N.Y., called Williamsburg. My dad was a cop who later became a New York City Narcotics Detective. He worked with guys you may know from movies and books like *The French Connection* and *Prince of the City.* When I was 12, my father died of a bullet wound to the chest. It was fired from his own gun as he sat in the front passenger seat of his unmarked squad car. He died just a few blocks from where he grew up in Brooklyn.

His death was deemed a suicide, but soon after, evidence surfaced that suggested foul play. However, the police department maintained it was a suicide and they denied his pension to my mother. Life changed forever for my mom, my younger sister and me that day.

I experienced so much pain about his death for more than 25 years. Then I had an unexpected session with a then unknown medium named John Edward. He would later become famous because of a television show called *Crossing Over.* He also wrote several books. He explained to me in great detail how my father was murdered and how police corruption played a big part in his death. Later, two other mediums confirmed the story exactly as John Edward had described it to me.

So my journey into the spiritual and metaphysical world started early. It actually began with my father's death, a powerful karmic event in my life.

I was always interested in self-improvement, psychology and bettering myself. After experiencing two business bankruptcies by the age of 30, I was desperate to make changes.

I was ready and willing to do whatever was necessary to facilitate change. This sent me on a journey into the depths of my soul. Along the way, I met powerful healers, gifted psychics, mediums and enlightened masters. I discovered that the most powerful forces in the universe are energy, emotion, beliefs, fear and love. I undertook deep introspective work, heightened levels of awareness, meditation and experienced intense emotion.

As I began to apply the principles I will share with you in this book, my life began to change. It started with a heightened sense of awareness. I was feeling much better and more relaxed. Even when things in the outside world were slow to change, I knew I was elevating my energy because I felt completely different than I had before.

I started to share what I was learning with others and a new mission emerged. I changed from a hardcore New York businessman/salesman to a spiritual teacher and healer. My life would never be the same. Each day has become a miracle. I am honored to share this information with you and hope it helps you create the life you came here to experience.

Your New Definition of Karma

I have always found it easier to work with principles when I break them down. This is how I have gained a greater understanding. Simplicity has also been a valuable teaching tool that helps others digest the information in useable pieces. This makes it easier to retain and apply the principles in real life.

My new definition of karma…

> *Your karma is the blueprint for the emotional work you came to experience in this lifetime.*

As a result, your karma is the driving force in your life.

Think of karma as your map. Everything in the universe is energy. That means your karma is energy as well. Right now you are holding the energy in your Chakra Energy System (you will learn more about this in chapter six) as emotion, feelings and beliefs. Your karma is the unresolved feelings and emotions you came here to experience in this lifetime.

You are creating your life on a moment-by-moment basis based on the feelings and emotions you came here to experience. Notice I said you are *creating* your life. This is a major piece of the puzzle. To move forward you must see yourself as the creator of your life. This means you must accept the fact that you are creating everything in your life 24/7 … without exception. When something wonderful happens … you did it. When something terrible happens … you did it.

In the world of energy, there is no such thing as good and bad. All experiences are designed to help us deal with the emotional issues we are here to experience. Here on earth we need the polarity of good and bad, right and wrong. We are living this human experience, and feelings are the name of the game.

I would love to say I am above it all and do not judge anything, but living as a human being makes that virtually impossible. We are always judging ourselves and others. It is a huge part of human existence. If I say *"I love your shoes,"* I am, in effect, judging your shoes. The key is being aware of your negative judgment and criticism. Negativity blocks energy and slows your progress.

Are you always judging others in a negative way? Maybe you are jealous of a friend or think your boss is incompetent. Maybe you judge those who are wealthy or famous. Be aware of this type of judgment. Negative energy gets in your way and makes moving forward with this program more difficult. If you are living in a state of highly negative judgment, you are living with an extreme feeling of self-hatred. I know this well. I lived with this for many years.

Some people resist the concept that they are the creators of everything in their lives. It takes great courage to accept that you have so much power. We are much more comfortable being victims and feeling weak. Living in a state of weakness is easier because it removes your ability to make changes. As a victim, you have no power and cannot change what is.

We all feel like we're victims sometimes. No matter how much we try to avoid it, there will be times when we feel like we are getting a raw deal. We often feel we are at the mercy of government, employers, society and the system in general.

There are some people who accept full responsibility, but still feel they are victims. How can I be a victim if I am taking responsibility for my life? I can live as a martyr. In this case I accept my circumstances, but I do not see myself as having any power. It is the classic "poor me" situation. I accept my life in a self-sacrificing manner.

The key to being the creator of your life is accepting that you have the power to make changes. You must know you are the one with your hands on the steering wheel. Accepting this power means accepting the responsibility for everything in your life. Most people fear this type of power. For this reason, many would rather live as victims and martyrs.

You are creating your life based on the feelings and emotions your soul wants you to feel. This is your karma. To have a full life experience, you must feel the entire spectrum of emotions. If there is no fear or sadness, how can you experience love and joy? You would not know the difference. Swings of emotion are important in your journey. Accept this fact and embrace every emotional aspect of your human experience. This is the reason you're here in the first place – to feel your emotions.

What Your Karma Looks Like

To bust your karma you have to know how to identify it. You have to be able to see and understand it. This is the **awareness step** of the process. Without awareness it is impossible to move your life forward. It is important to realize, though, that awareness can also be a trap. You may begin to believe that once you are aware of something you can control it. This is the trap you want to avoid.

Many people are very *aware* of their destructive behavior, but still can't seem to stop it. Nowhere is this more evident than with addictions. All addicts, regardless of type, knows that continuing along their current path will lead to the destruction of themselves and others. And yet, they still can't seem to stop themselves. Why? This is all part of that person's karmic journey.

Doing this work requires you to throw logic out the window. As human beings, we have a difficult time understanding self-destructive behavior. You must understand that you are not here to be self-destructive; you are here to *feel* what being self-destructive feels like. This will manifest in your emotions and addictions to specific feelings.

We are all addicted to certain feelings. These feelings represent the core karmic issues we are here to resolve. You will be addicted to feeling a certain way based on how you grew up and what you are accustomed to feeling.

If you grew up in an emotionally abusive household, you may be addicted to feeling like a victim. Notice I said the *feeling* of being a victim. Your karma is about the *feeling*, not the *action*. If you came here to *feel* this feeling of being a victim, you will select parents and a circumstance that will create that feeling (I will discuss the selection of your parents in chapter three).

You will have the desire to feel sorry for yourself and to feel victimized. This is the feeling or karma you are here to experience. Once again, there is no logic here. This is not happening on a conscious level. This feeling is now coded to your DNA. No matter what action you take, you always end up feeling like a victim.

This subconscious feeling becomes the driving force in your life. In this case, you will always have the desire to feel like a victim. This becomes your normal way of living and you continue to recreate the feeling you desire. You have actually become addicted to feeling like a victim and you can't live without that feeling.

Eliminating this feeling creates great distress for you. This is no different than an addiction to drugs or alcohol. What happens to an addict when you take away their drug of choice? They go through withdrawal and feel great discomfort.

The same thing is going to happen to you as you let go of your emotional addiction.

Each individual came to experience different feelings. Some came to feel lonely, others to experience physical illness or financial struggles. There are those who want to feel the feelings of having great power or celebrity status. As you can see, we can experience the gamut of emotions and experiences. There is no good or bad karma. There is only the journey you are here to experience.

The energy of your karma is held in your Chakra System until you feel the feelings and release the energy. Once all the layers of the emotion are released and your soul is satisfied, the karma in that specific area is busted. This applies to the specific issue you are working on. Once the energy is cleared, the desire to feel the feeling you are addicted to is no longer there. The same thing happens regardless of the feeling you are here to experience such as loneliness, physical illness or financial struggle. The desire to feel the specific feeling will be gone and you will stop recreating it.

Then you can move on to the next feeling. Isn't that exciting? No worries. By the time you are finished here, you will be ready to deal with each new issue as it is created. Yes, you are creating it.

Clearing Your Karma

Clearing your karma requires you to feel your feelings to release the negative energy you are holding. When I was first introduced to this concept, I was confused and bewildered.

What did it mean to *feel my feelings?*

Wasn't I already feeling my feelings?

How was feeling something releasing negative energy?

Why was this necessary for me to create a successful business and generate more money?

These were some of the questions I had as I began the karma busting process. Most people have not been trained or conditioned to truly *feel* emotions. Frequently we were taught to repress or ignore feelings.

The first step is realizing that you have not been feeling your true emotions. The other issue is that you have been repressing or blocking your emotions for a long time. You can't just flip a switch and start feeling again. Once again, this is about accepting and moving forward. It does not matter how repressed you are. It is always possible to open up your energy and emotion!

I am a kid from Brooklyn who started his career as a truck driver. Expressing my feelings was not exactly high on the priority list in my home. If I can do this … anyone can!

How were feelings and emotions dealt with in your home? Your answer to this question will tell you the extent of your repression. Some families are better than others when dealing with emotions, but we all had some amount of negativity regarding expressing our emotions growing up. You may have been criticized for being too emotional. Or, if you grew up in a hostile emotional environment, you might have repressed your feelings in order to survive. After years of conditioning, it takes some time to open up.

The best way to begin the process is to simply be more aware of how you are feeling during the day. The key here is allowing yourself to feel what you truly feel – without judgment. This can be very challenging, especially when you have a negative feeling about a person or situation. Maybe you have a new co-worker who is receiving a lot of attention. You realize you feel jealous and upset. What would you ordinarily do with that feeling?

In most cases, you would find a friend at work who agrees with you – validation. Or you might try to make the new person feel uncomfortable. This is not dealing with your feelings. You have been conditioned to push, or project, your feelings onto others. Every time you do this, the energy that brought up the jealousy stays with you. In this case, you have the desire to feel jealousy but you won't let yourself go there.

Why?

Because the true feeling lies under the jealousy. This is the emotion you are trying desperately to avoid. Acting out and pushing away are defense mechanisms for avoiding true feelings.

Why do you want to run from the true feeling?

It's simple. You want to avoid the emotional pain of feeling it.

This is a natural defense mechanism and part of human DNA. We are designed to avoid pain. To move forward, you need to jump into the pain and feel it. This is the exact opposite of what we are conditioned to do. You must be willing to go into a dark place and feel your true feelings to bust your karma.

Every time you feel the deeper emotion, you release the energy. This dissolves the feeling and diminishes the desire to repeat the behavior.

Uncovering the Truth

This was an area of great struggle for me. I had a difficult time identifying my feelings and then going deeper. Once again, I am going to break this into pieces to make it easier and more "user friendly."

Imagine your feelings and emotions existing on two levels.

Level 1: Surface emotions – Feelings that get your attention.

Examples of surface emotions: fear, anger, jealousy, envy, animosity, resentment, guilt, insecurity, displeasure, disgust.

Level 2: Your true feelings – The pain below the surface emotion. These feelings are based in fear and on feeling unloved on some level.

Examples of true feelings: loneliness, unworthiness, feelings of unimportance, insignificance, failure, and just feeling you are 'no good.'

Let's go back to our previous example with the new employee. The surface emotion is jealousy. The moment you feel it, there is a surge of energy. What you do with this initial feeling is the key to making progress. As a karma buster, you know the feeling must be dealt with on a deeper level. The surface emotion of jealousy is helping you get to the true feeling. It is **not** about the new employee getting attention. It's about you!

As the creator of your life, you know you have great power and can never be a victim. We create situations to help us bring up buried feelings. You should actually thank the person who upset you because they are helping you move to a higher level of awareness and enlightenment.

The first question you must ask yourself going forward is:

Why did I create this now?

This is where the work becomes a bit more challenging. Now you have to go deeper and uncover your true feelings. What emotion lies below the jealousy and why is it bothering you? Don't worry if you get stuck at this point in the beginning. Moving into these deeper feelings is new to you and it will take time to adjust.

All of your deeper feelings and emotions are anchored in your childhood. In this example, you would ask yourself "*who made me feel jealous as a child?*" These strong emotions will always be linked to your parents. Each feeling will be connected to one of them.

I was working with a client (let's call him Nick), who had a lot of issues with jealousy. He always felt he was being passed over at work and not receiving the credit he deserved. As we delved deeper, he realized he had an issue with his younger sister. He felt that his father gave all of his attention to her growing up. This made Nick jealous of his sister, but he was actually holding the negative energy and anger toward his father.

The next step is feeling the real feeling. In Nick's case, it started with jealousy, then progressed to anger (another surface emotion) and finally we uncovered the true feeling of Nick feeling unloved. Nick did not receive the love and attention he desired from his father. It made him feel uncared for and unimportant.

We are conditioned not to see our parents in a negative light. The key to clearing your negative energy is feeling your feelings without judgment. Recognize that you are not upset with your parent (though on some level you are). You are actually upset with how they made you feel. This will make it easier for you to get to the feeling and clear it.

Moving forward requires you to release your old energy. This is accomplished using an emotional regression meditation process. Next you will find one of the energy clearing meditations I have been using for many years. The examples cited are composites based on meditations created during many sessions with varied clients. They are not meant to represent any specific client.

Preparation for Your Meditation: Select a spot in your home and make it your meditation area. This helps build energy and makes the area special. Before you begin, be sure to select a time when you know you will not be interrupted or disturbed. Also, be sure you have time after the meditation to reflect and relax.

You must be sitting up, preferably on the floor. You can lean against a wall or chair for support. The important thing is not to lie down. When you lie down, your brain moves into sleep mode.

Have a box of tissues, water and a pad of paper and a pen nearby. Begin with deep breathing … in and out on a three count. This will help you relax and center your energy.

Meditation 1: Clearing Daily Issues

Focus on your day and go through the events that occurred. Did anything happen during the day that upset you? This does not have to be a major incident. It could be something as simple as a comment made by a co-worker or someone in the supermarket. If it brought up a strong feeling, there is work to be done on that specific emotion.

Bring the incident into your mind and see it as if you were watching a movie. Make sure you are emotionally connected to the feeling you were experiencing at the moment. Keep replaying the incident until you can identify the feeling. This may trigger a memory of an incident that happened in your past. The past incident is where the anchoring emotion is being held. You may not be able to go this deep in the beginning. Eventually, you will link the incident to an emotional issue from your childhood.

Allow yourself to feel the emotions from your childhood. These are the feelings you were not allowed to feel at the time. Do not attempt to be logical or judge the feelings. Simply allow the emotions to flow through you. Allow yourself to cry or become upset if this is how you truly feel. Continue to replay the incident from your past and keep reliving the experience. Stay in the feeling for as long as it takes to release the energy.

Every time you feel a feeling on a deep level, negative energy is released. This is how you are clearing your karma, by feeling it. This may sound simplistic, but most people live in a state of deep repression/denial and do not feel their true emotions at all. As energy is released, you begin to create a different vibration of internal energy which creates different levels of attraction.

If the same feeling comes up again, repeat the process and release the energy. How do you release the energy? You release the energy by allowing yourself to feel the feeling. Every time you release negative energy, you are elevating your vibration. Each feeling that comes up is linked to something in your past.

Example of Live Group Session 1: Student – Grant

After completing the group meditation, we encourage people to share their experience. By sharing, they are helping themselves by talking about their feelings and, in the process, they are helping others know they are not alone. As you would expect, some people are very open while others choose to remain silent.

The first thing I ask people to do is describe the issue or incident they brought up in the meditation. Then we begin to talk about the feelings.

Grant: My incident happened today. I started a new job selling cable subscriptions door to door. The incident occurred at my third stop of the day. An older man answered the door. I introduced myself and started to tell him about the service. He put his hand up and told me to stop talking. He said he was not interested.

Joe: What bothered you about this incident?

Grant: It was the way he dismissed me.

Joe: What did you feel at that moment?

Grant: I was really angry at the guy. He was so disrespectful and rude. So I would say I was angry.

Joe: Anger is not really the feeling. It is a surface emotion. How did he make you feel?

Grant: I am telling you I was angry – really *mad* – as I walked away from the house.

Joe: I know you were angry, but how did you feel about what happened?

Note: We went back and forth for a while on this one.

Grant: I really felt like I had no value, like I was piece of shit.

Joe: Now we are getting to the feeling. How did this feel on an emotional level?

At this point Grant became very emotional. His eyes welled up with tears and he was visibly upset.

Grant: I felt like a real loser at that moment .... walking around, knocking on doors and having people reject me all day. It was a terrible feeling. No one was interested in what I had to say.

Joe: Who made you feel this way as a child?

A long hesitation followed.

Grant: My dad never paid attention to me and was very dismissive. He made me feel like a loser. That guy made me feel the exact same way as I stood at the door.

Joe: So what was the feeling you experienced?

Grant: I felt completely unworthy… like I had no value at all as a person.

The feeling overwhelmed Grant and he started to cry. He was feeling the deep pain he had been repressing for many years. As he cried, he was releasing the painful energy he had never expressed.

He was beginning to release this deep emotion and intense feeling of unworthiness. These were powerful negative emotions he had been holding toward his father since childhood. Linking the present incident to the past was the key to Grant feeling his true emotions.

In the beginning of the conversation, you will notice how Grant insisted he was angry and was unable to get to the real feeling. Then he started to project his anger onto the man at the door. Most people get stuck right there. As a result, the deeper feeling is never addressed and the energy remains trapped in your body.

Moving forward will require that you move past the surface emotion and get to the true feeling. Yes, Grant was *angry* but that was not the feeling. We have not been properly trained to identify our feelings. We may say I am *angry* or *sad*, but we are not identifying the deeper feeling that often accompanies this surface emotion.

We were going back and forth until Grant moved past the initial anger and advanced into the true feeling. He sensed there was deep emotional pain in the situation and he wanted to avoid it. This is a natural defense mechanism. We are designed to avoid pain.

Clearing your negative energy requires you to move into the painful feelings you have been trying to avoid your entire life.

How Will You Know the Energy Has Been Cleared?

You release negative energy by feeling your feelings on a deep emotional level. Every time you allow yourself to feel, a piece of the energy is released. Your deeper emotional scars are layered. As a result, you will not be able to release all the energy at once. You will have to deal with the same feeling many times before you can release all the energy and clear the karma. When you no longer have a strong emotional reaction to a particular incident, you will know the energy has been cleared.

Grant was holding deep emotional pain centered around the feeling of unworthiness. This went back to the way his father made him feel as a child. As new situations arise, Grant will no longer feel the same emotional charge. He may still feel unworthiness at times, but at a much lower level of intensity. In addition, he will no longer have the desire to feel the feeling of unworthiness and he will stop creating those situations for himself.

You will notice the same thing with your feelings as you do karma busting work.

IMPORTANT NOTE: No Judgment or Projecting, Please

When you are releasing energy, it is natural to move into judgment and projection. Grant was upset with his father. It is natural to have a negative or even hateful feeling for the person who caused you pain. You must allow yourself to accept these feelings. If you feel strong feelings of hate or anger toward a parent, you must make it okay in your mind. These are your true feelings. They are not good or bad, right or wrong. They are your core truths.

Do not judge the feeling or the person. When you judge, you move into thinking rather than feeling, and you fall into victim mode. This will cause you to project your emotion onto the person or incident and move away from your core feelings. Stay with the feelings inside of you instead of projecting them out.

You may struggle with this in the beginning. We have a difficult time moving into full acceptance of our feelings. Give yourself time and stay with your emotions. Eventually you will move past judgment and right into how you truly feel.

Energy Transformation

Every time you have an emotional energy experience, you are transforming your DNA and karma. Your energy has been changed at a core level. This will change your energy vibration and begin to create new experiences in the outside world. It takes some time for your energy to adjust after an emotional release.

After a deep emotion clearing episode, you will feel drained. This is normal as you have just released energy you have been holding for a long time. You may feel flu-like symptoms, body aches and general lethargy. Do not be alarmed when this happens. You have gone though a dramatic transformation. Your physical body and energy field will require some time to adjust. This is the time to nurture yourself back to full strength.

In addition, you may also feel a bit dizzy or foggy at times. This is also part of the transformational energy process. Emotions are the driving force in all of our lives and they are extremely powerful.

Snapshot of the Karma Busting Process

Step 1. **Awareness:** Be aware of your feelings all day long.

Step 2. **Trigger:** Someone or something will trigger a strong feeling.

Step 3. **Identify the Surface Emotion:** What did you feel?

Step 4. **Use Meditation 1:** Clearing Daily Issues.

Step 5. **Repeat the Process.**

Charting Your Emotions

People are always asking me how they can do a better job identifying surface emotions to get to the deeper true feelings. Here is a simple process that will help you do this. I like to call it *Emotional Identification.*

When you feel a charge of emotion, follow this sequence.

1. Ask yourself: *What am I* ***really*** *feeling right now?*
2. For example, answer: *Anger (surface emotion).* Then ask yourself *Why is this person or situation making me angry?*

3. Answer: *He or she is making me feel unworthy.* This is the true feeling, unworthiness.
4. Ask yourself: *Who made me feel this way as a child?*

By holding yourself in the feeling and not projecting, it will be much easier to identify the true feeling. Be aware and follow this sequence. It takes time to make it an automatic habit.

2 Your Karmic Wheel

Ultimately, your objective is to get off your Karmic Wheel so you can break your negative cycles of karma. I learned this energy concept many years ago. Most of us would see this as a pattern of behavior. You are actually holding and recycling the same energy or karma over and over again. When you break the cycle, you get off the Karmic Wheel and stop repeating the same patterns.

You are, in effect, creating your future based on your past. Let's say you have always struggled in your relationships. This is your cycle/karma in this area. As a result, you are holding fear and do not believe or trust that any relationship will work. Since this is the feeling you are holding, you have repeated this cycle over and over again. By now it makes perfect sense not to trust or believe in a loving relationship. This is because you have never experienced one. You will continue to recreate this episode until you break your Karmic Wheel in this area.

The Karmic Wheel

The Karmic Wheel is trapped energy that cycles through your system attracting similar people and situations. When the emotions attached to a specific cycle are not resolved, the cycle begins again. ***Your destructive patterns are being driven by unresolved emotional issues from your past.***

Seeing Your Cycles

Knowing your patterns or cycles depends upon your level of awareness. Even people who are very aware have trouble identifying some of their deeper patterns. As you shift the way you see the world, it will become much easier to detect and break these deep negative energy cycles. Try to see everything as an energetic cycle or wheel. You will be amazed at the patterns you are replaying again and again.

Example: Approval-Seeking Cycle

People have an overwhelming desire to receive love from their parents. When we do not receive the love we desire, it is natural to seek it elsewhere.

Your cycle always begins with desire. To identify your Karmic Wheel, you must identify the desire that is driving your behavior. In the parental love example, the desire is that you want someone to love and appreciate you. Everyone has the desire to be loved, but the intensity of this desire is based on the amount of love you received as a child.

We begin with identifying the desire: *I want people to approve of me, love me and appreciate me.* The cycle always begins with attraction. In the negative energy of approval seeking, I am actually attracting people who will ***not*** approve of me. You read it right – people who will not approve of me. Why would you attract people who will not approve of you when you think you are seeking approval? This is because your parents did not give you the love or approval you desired. So you are going to replay the cycle with a new person.

Wow! Take a moment and absorb that one.

This cycle is now a part of your Karmic Wheel or pattern. It was established long ago, based on the emotions you are here to experience.

You attract a new friend and your desire is to receive approval. This desire sparks a feeling in you. In this case, you are feeling the fear of not receiving approval. You can't have that … so you jump into action.

You may buy gifts, drive your friend to the airport and babysit his or her kids – all in an effort to receive the approval you are seeking. When you barely receive a thank you for all of your efforts, the desire intensifies … and you do more!

I have seen people over-extend themselves for years in an effort to receive this feeling of love. The person on the other end of the relationship, the one you attracted, will not give you the approval or love you seek. Why not? You are doing everything in your power to get their attention. In reality, on a deep emotional level, you do not want the approval or love. You are trapped in the cycle of feeling unloved and, because of that, you keep on playing it out with different people.

I know this may sound contradictory, but on an energy level, it makes perfect sense. You are consciously seeking approval and take action accordingly. On a subconscious energy level, you are really seeking disapproval. So you attract a person to make you feel bad about yourself. This is the replay of emotions you were feeling as a child.

Those feelings make you upset with your "friend" and you project your anger onto them. This judgment moves you into feeling like a victim. You get to feel bad, sad, weak and unworthy (just like you did at home). In most cases you will find some friends or family members to validate your story, agree with you and your wheel is complete.

You may also continue to play out the same cycles with your parents. This is natural because your relationship with them is based on the Karmic Wheel. You may still be seeking approval from them as an adult. People continually recreate the wheel with family members and revert to childlike patterns.

In this example, no feelings or emotional issues were resolved. Now you can start the cycle all over again. And so it goes…

Breaking the Karmic Wheel

You have to see and accept your wheel to break it. If you resist or make excuses for yourself or blame others, you are certain to remain stuck. You have to be very aware of your desires and catch the cycle early to break it.

Karmic Wheel Cycle

1. **Desire:** You have a desire to feel a specific feeling. In the new friend example, it was approval-seeking. All of your desires are based on receiving love. All of your attraction and action is driven by this powerful feeling.
2. **Attraction:** You attract people and situations based on how you are feeling about yourself. Remember, this has nothing to do with what you want consciously.
3. **Action:** You take action and over-extend yourself based on your desire.
4. **Becoming a Victim:** Eventually you realize you are not going to receive love and you move into victim mode. Then you project your anger onto others. You feel taken advantage of and abused.
5. **Seeking Validation:** You have a strong desire to be right. It is important to receive validation from others to ease your pain. You seek out people to confirm your feelings.

Then You Start Over and Begin the Cycle Again

As you can see, there are a number of steps to each cycle. As you practice, your awareness will improve and you will have the ability to identify your cycle earlier ... and to stop it.

Draw Your Own Karmic Wheel

Seeing the visual will help you break the cycle.

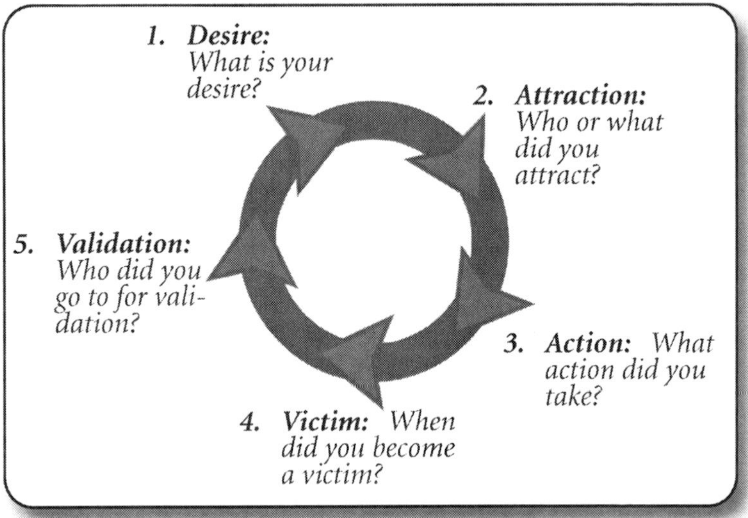

Now that you are aware and see your Karmic Wheel, it is time to break it. Different feelings create different wheels but many emotions overlap. Clearing one major emotion will help you across the board. Energy is not linear. What you feel extends to all areas of your life. Breaking the cycle will have an impact in all areas of your life.

Time for Opposite Action

As described earlier, awareness is the first step, but it is also a trap. Once you identify your cycle, you have to stop it. You accomplish this by employing *opposite action.*

What is opposite action? Doing the opposite of what you would normally do. This is actually a lot more difficult than it sounds.

Let's still use the example of approval-seeking because it is such a big issue for so many people. In this feeling, you are going to attract a person who needs something. You receive a phone call and "your friend" asks for a ride to the airport. Your normal reaction, because you desire approval, is to run out the door, keys in hand.

Now you are a karma buster!

So instead of running out the door to do this favor, your normal behavior, you are going to say *NO!* This is the essence of opposite action.

~Stop ...
for a moment and imagine how it will feel to actually say *'no'* in this situation. Close the book and sit with the feeling for a while ...

Welcome back! So how did you feel? If you are like most people, you experienced a strong feeling of guilt. You felt like you were a 'bad' person for not doing this favor. Regardless of your circumstances, you feel this was a 'bad' thing to do. You see yourself as a good person only when you are extending yourself to others.

Our emotional work requires you to feel the guilt of saying no and make it okay. This is very challenging at first. It is so 'not you' to act this way. Changing energy at this core level requires commitment and the willingness to choose a different path.

When you do what is best for yourself, you are in a state of self love. The old you would have gone out of your way, driven your friend to the airport, not received a thank you and returned home feeling like a victim. Now you are living in a state of self love. This is not your normal state ... yet. In the beginning it will feel uncomfortable. You will feel selfish and guilty as you move into this new energy. You must continue along this path until the feeling of self love becomes your normal state. It takes time. Be patient and realize that in this frantic state of approval seeking, you were never going to receive the love you were seeking.

You cannot bust your Karmic Wheel if you continue to react the same way. Opposite action is challenging, especially in the early stages. Your family and friends are used to you acting and reacting in a certain way. Suddenly you are powerful and filled with a new vibration of positive energy. As the Beach Boys' song stated, you will have *Good Vibrations.*

Be ready. You are sure to face criticism and some emotional attacks as you move into this new energy. As your Karmic Wheel crumbles, you are shattering the old energy dynamics involving your family and friends.

You will know you are doing well when…

1. People start asking "*is there something wrong with you?*"
2. People start telling you how much you have changed.
3. You begin to receive disapproval from family and friends.
4. Your family and friends plan an intervention.

When #4 happens, you know you have arrived!

I am giving you this information to prepare you for what is coming. It is difficult to hold your ground when everyone seems to be against you. In reality, you are exposing their fears by changing the status quo.

Be strong and keep on loving yourself. As you do, your Karmic Wheel will be busted and a new positive cycle will begin.

3 Why You Selected Your Parents

You actually selected your parents before you arrived here on earth. *"Oh my! Why would I select **them**?"* I hear this type of comment every day.

This is a very difficult concept for some people to accept. It is hard to imagine selecting parents who were physically, emotionally or mentally abusive. Once again, this does not make sense logically. However, you must understand and be open to this concept to move forward with this process. You came here to experience these emotions and have these experiences.

Each person selected specific parents because they had the best DNA code, genetics and karmic energy for the emotional work they came to do in this lifetime. A person may select a father who was verbally abusive, for example. Why would someone select this father? Because that person came to experience, and then clear, the feeling attached to being verbally abused. This would be one of the many emotions linked back to karmic energy. In this life people have the opportunity to feel those feelings and resolve their emotional issues.

Once you accept this concept, you can begin to break down your feelings and emotions. It is more challenging for some people than others, especially for those of us who did not grow up in nurturing and loving environments.

One of our greatest challenges is accepting that we are exactly like the parent we can't stand. Your father may have been very selfish and you hate that quality. Now you find yourself acting in the exact same manner.

There is a ton of judgment involved when we are dealing with parents. How many times have you said, "I do not want to be *anything* like my mother?" Then you realize you have characteristics exactly like some of hers ... oh my! Accepting your similarities is the key to breaking the energy and karma.

Energetically your parents are perfect for the emotional work you are here to conquer. As you look at your parents, you will begin to see traits you are duplicating. In most cases, you will be more like one parent than the other (although you will have traits from both). On a percentage basis, it may be something like a 70/30 percent or 60/40 percent.

The easiest way to uncover these true emotions and see your true self is to take a deeper look at each parent from an emotional perspective. Look at each of your parents based on traits and feelings.

Begin with positive traits, such as *organized, intelligent* and *responsive to your needs.* Then move into the negative traits: *unreliable, selfish* and *poor at communicating.* Next, move into feelings. How did each parent make you feel as a child? List as many feelings as possible. Did you feel *loved, nurtured* and *safe*? Did you feel *fearful, terrified* and *unsafe*?

This exercise will help you uncover your true feelings about your childhood and help you expose the emotions and pain you are currently carrying. Use the charts on the next page to create lists of parental personality traits. As you look at these lists, look at yourself. How many of these traits and emotions are you holding onto right now? It is amazing to see how deep these feelings and emotions run. Bringing childhood emotions into your awareness is a great tool as you move through the karma busting process.

Mom

Positive Traits	Negative Traits	Positive Feelings	Negative Feelings

Dad

Positive Traits	Negative Traits	Positive Feelings	Negative Feelings

Different Kids = Different Experiences

People frequently say, "*I raised my kids exactly the same and yet they are completely different.*" This, of course, is not true. It is impossible to raise children the same, but parents usually tell this story to make themselves feel better. An only child receives 100% of the parents' attention. The minute a second child is born, the attention is split. Usually this is not going to be an equal split because a newborn baby requires more attention than a two year old.

All of a sudden the two year went from receiving 100% of the attention to 25% .... ouch! This has an emotional impact on the two year old. The newborn could never receive 100% of the attention because a sibling was already in place in the family. So immediately the children's experiences on an emotional level are completely different.

Each person also is born with different emotional issues to resolve. This creates a unique genetic split. You may be 70/30, with more of the energy of your mother. Your sibling may be the opposite and have 70% your father's energy. Remember, this genetic make-up is all based on the emotions and feelings each of you came here to experience.

Then we have what I like to call the "click factor." Certain people just click better with certain people. This is also true of parents and their kids. It makes sense to click more with the person who shares similar energy. No parent wants to admit this, but it is absolutely true. Let's say a father has two sons and one is a sports nut while the other loves music. The dad is a sports fanatic who has little interest in music. Which son will click better with Dad?

These two boys are going to grow up in the same home with very different experiences. Neither experience is better or worse. Each experience is simply different. Yet one brother may grow up feeling slighted or dismissed. These are valid feelings that are part of his karma.

Now you must examine how your experience has, and is, affecting your life. How do you feel about the treatment you received at home? Do you feel you were supported or ignored? Were you loved or made to feel unimportant? Are you still carrying these feelings today? All of these feelings are part of the karmic energy you are here to clear.

Your Family Karma

Your karma is anchored in the feelings and emotions of your childhood family. Dealing with relationships in your family will always be challenging. In some cases you can resolve issues and, in others, you may be unable to do so. Family issues are one more thing you will have to learn to accept as you expand your energy and break the Karmic Wheel.

How you were treated and made to feel at home is a major part of this karma busting journey. Your energy is tied to what you learned at home. Growing up you absorbed the energy of your home. The feelings you absorbed created your belief system and patterns or cycles of behavior. Now you need to break these cycles at the core level of energy.

It's time to examine your relationships and behavioral patterns from childhood. Begin with the relationship you had (and may still have) with your mother and father. How were you treated? What was expected of you? The expectation level placed upon you is very important. Your desire, as a child, was to make your parents happy. You attempted to accomplish this by doing the things you were made to believe made you good. When you did the things your parents labeled as good, you received the approval you were seeking. You may not have really received it, but on some level you felt you did.

As a child, I was conditioned to over-extend myself and go out of my way for others. This was expected of me. I never received love in return, but I was conditioned to over-extend myself and go out of my way for others. This started my cycle of over-extending and expecting nothing in return. This feeling led me into two bankruptcies! My childhood pattern was to do a lot and expect nothing in return. In a later chapter I will discuss the "art of receiving" in more detail.

Look at your patterns and beliefs. Are you still playing them out today? Are you still doing this with your family? Have you brought in new people to repeat the same cycle? This is all part of your karma.

Moving forward requires you to know and accept yourself on all levels. Be aware of your family karma and use the opposite action technique outlined in the last chapter. Breaking the family karma is challenging because you are going to feel like a 'bad' person as you make this transition and move off the Karmic Wheel.

In addition to busting your own karma, you are also disrupting the family karma. Regardless of how dysfunctional your family may be, they will desperately attempt to cling to their old patterns and cycles. They cannot continue their old patterns without you. When you break the energy, a chain reaction is created.

You are leaving your old role and releasing karma. Now all the other players have to make adjustments. This disrupts family dynamics and begins to shatter the family Karmic Wheel. On a deeper energy level, they feel tremendous disruption and panic. What are they going to do now? You have left the family drama and moved to a new place.

This change forces family members to look at themselves in an entirely new way. They will resist at first, and some may never come around, but they all feel the shift of energy.

My family was very upset when I busted my karma and broke their wheel. I gave up my role as the reliable caretaker and peacemaker. This created great resentment toward me. I was taking opposite action and it was uncomfortable on both sides. There were long periods of time when we did not speak to or see each other. It is very challenging to hold your ground under this type of emotional pressure. I also felt deep feelings of guilt and failure as I moved through this process.

You must understand how your new behavior looks from your family's perspective, especially when you are dealing with people at lower levels of awareness and understanding. (This is not a judgment – it is an observation.) As you move through your karma busting work, you will see how some people are open and aware. Others are resistant. This is based on their level of fear. People who are very fear based do not like change of any kind. It is for this reason they remain stuck for most, or all, of their lives.

Once again you must move into the feeling of self love.

Meditation 2: Cleaning Out the Basement

I call this meditation *cleaning out the basement* because it deals with the deep, older feelings you are holding onto about your parents. Please understand that ultimately you are holding the energy yourself, but here, in the third dimensional world, we seem to direct it toward one or both parents.

The preparation is the same as Meditation #1, but in this case you are going to remember back to your childhood. When doing this meditation, you will focus on one parent at a time. Select the parent you want to work on before you begin. This will help you focus your energy. You may want to look at a photo of yourself as a child and a picture of this parent before you begin to bring up the feelings.

See yourself as a child, going back as far as you can. The more details you can recall the better. All details are good ... what you are wearing, hair style, shoes. There is no right or wrong age. Some people can go all the way back to infancy, while others are more blocked regarding their childhood.

Next, bring yourself into the home where you grew up. This will trigger an immediate feeling about the energy of your home. See yourself in the home and feel it. What are you feeling as you see yourself back in this place? Allow these feelings to settle in for a while. It is important to be in a state of feeling and not thinking.

Now, bring the parent you are focusing on into the room. What is the first feeling that comes up for you? How did this person make you feel as a child? There will be many emotions, but some strong feelings should jump out at you. In most cases, this will trigger the memory of a specific event from your childhood.

Allow yourself to move into the event and watch it play out. Remember, do not judge or use logic to understand or justify the situation. You must feel the feeling to release the deep pain you are holding.

This meditation will bring up many feelings including shame, guilt, unworthiness, fear, anger, desperation and panic, among others. Do not block the feeling … really "feel it" as deeply as possible. As you feel it, energy is released and your vibration is elevated. You may cry, become upset or move into a feeling of deep sadness. Keep replaying the particular scenario until you no longer feel upset.

Session #2: Amanda

In this meditation, I begin by asking people which parent they chose to work on. Then we move into feelings and emotions that come up in the process. In most cases people will cite a specific incident or incidents that occurred with that particular parent.

Amanda: I focused on my mother. My father and mother split right after I was born. I never really saw him and he did not help my mother financially. We were always struggling and moving from place to place. My mother was always stressed and did not pay much attention to me. I remembered a specific incident when she was upset with me about a mess I left in the kitchen. I was six years old at the time. She stormed out and left me alone for hours. When she returned, I went to hug her and she shrugged me off in a dismissive manner.

As an adult I have always felt sorry for her. She had a tough life and did the best she could. I did not want to see her in a negative light.

Joe: What was the feeling you had as a child in your home?

Amanda: I felt very nervous, panicky and unsafe. I felt I had let my mother down and was a bad kid.

Joe: How do you feel about your mother and the fact that she left you alone at age six?

Amanda: I understand she had to work and, in many cases, there was no one available to watch me.

Joe: That is not my question. I asked you how you felt about your mother leaving you alone in this manner.

Note: This is where a lot of people have resistance. They do not want to see a parent in a negative light. Instead of dealing with the feeling, Amanda moved into justification. When you justify, you are not allowing yourself to feel your emotions.

Once again we went back and forth for a while before Amanda was able to begin to move into her feelings about this painful issue.

Amanda: It made me feel unsafe and unwanted?

Joe: We are getting there, but how do you feel about your mother? She left you alone in an apartment, feeling unsafe, when you were six years old.

Amanda: I just started to feel some anger about this and now I feel unwanted. She made me feel like I was a burden and the cause of all of her problems. I felt so guilty and responsible for her pain. I hate her for that!

Joe: Allow yourself to really feel that feeling. What does it feel like?

Amanda: I feel like a horrible person, unworthy of any love or understanding.

This was a true emotional breakthrough for Amanda. She realized how her mother projected all of her sadness and unworthiness on to her. Amanda had repressed these feelings and protected her mother her entire life. She never came face to face with the true feelings she was holding.

All of a sudden, Amanda burst into tears and began to cry uncontrollably. This was truly a deep release of powerful feelings that had been repressed for many years.

Amanda was facing tremendous issues of trust and she always felt undeserving. As an adult she found herself moving constantly and she was unable to establish a steady romantic relationship. This was the result of these deep feelings she had been holding. Now she can begin the journey of healing herself as she releases these deep feelings and accepts the truth about how she felt as a child. Now she can see how it is affecting her present circumstance.

Drama vs. Feelings

I am Italian in this lifetime, so I know all about drama. People are always telling me how emotional they are and how they cry all the time. This does not mean you are feeling your feelings. Just because you cry at a movie does not mean you know how to feel your emotions.

You probably also know people who are given to emotional outbursts and, in some cases, they might even dramatically throw things at you. These people are not feeling anything either. They are acting out and being dramatic, but there isn't a true feeling within a hundred miles of them.

When you move into drama, there are no true feelings present. You know you are in drama when you are projecting your feelings onto others by judging, blaming or having a strong desire to be right.

Often an emotional outburst is how an individual manages stress. This provides temporary relief and diminishes the stress for the moment. As stress re-builds, they are sure to have another outburst to relieve the feeling again. This cycle will continue forever, as they never address the core feelings causing the stress in the first place.

You know you are truly connected to your feelings when you can identify and name the feeling. As discussed earlier, there are surface emotions and true feelings. The more you are tuned into your feelings, the easier this becomes. You must understand most of us were not taught or encouraged to feel our feelings.

Children are pure and automatically connect to how they really feel. Kids know how they feel all the time. If a child is upset, he or she reacts accordingly. Imagine yourself as a child during an emotional moment. Maybe you hurt yourself and came in, crying to your mother, and she tells you, "Don't be so dramatic. You are fine." She just invalidated your feeling and told you the feeling is wrong. This is where the disconnection of feelings begins for us.

As you were told not to feel a certain way or made to feel ashamed of your feelings, you lost the connection with your emotions. All of a sudden, you're 43 and have no idea how you truly feel.

Surface emotions – anger, jealousy, anxiety, fear and sadness – are examples of the emotions that come before the true feelings. If you are angry, ask yourself why am I feeling angry? This will help you uncover the true feeling. What is it about this person or situation that is bringing up the feeling of anger?

I was speaking to someone about his friend, who was very successful. He was telling me about a new house his friend was building. He felt it was unnecessary and 'over the top.' He was clearly feeling very jealous about his friend's success. As we went deeper, I asked him why his friend's success stirred up so much emotion. He soon realized he felt like a failure in his own life. That was his true feeling deep down. It had nothing to do with his friend's success. He was simply projecting the negative feelings about himself onto his friend.

4 Busting Out of Your Ego-Identity

Every person here on earth has, and requires, an ego-identity. This identity allows us to exist separately from source energy and live an individual life. We are all part of the same energy. To experience what we want to experience on this earth, we become separated from source energy and take on unique identities. This separation creates a feeling of shame. We all share this feeling. It is the true original sin. Every person carries a certain degree of shame. You feel shame because you left the source to have this life here on earth.

When you become more aware and connected to your spirit-self, your ego-identity becomes less important. You are not as concerned about what others are thinking or about maintaining a certain image. People who are very connected to their ego-identities carry dense energy. Those who are more spiritual carry lighter energy.

Celebrities and public figures are perfect examples of people holding strong ego-identities. They believe this identity is critical to becoming successful and powerful. Therefore, a tremendous amount of energy is used maintaining their public identities. Most people spend a lot of time and energy keeping their identities alive. Let's face it ... your ego-identity is who you think you are and you will do whatever it takes to protect yourself.

Please understand that you require an ego-identity to function here on earth. The key is balancing your ego-identity with your true spirit. This is a slippery slope, wrought with challenges and pitfalls. It is very easy for the negative ego to take over your life. The more you separate from your true self, the easier it is for the negative ego to gain control. Once the negative ego rules your life, all of your decisions and actions will become focused on keeping this identity alive and well.

We see this happen regularly in the world of business. As a person becomes more successful, powerful and rich, it is natural to want even more. At some point it is no longer about the money. The negative ego has taken over and has an insatiable desire to be fed. The negative ego is now being driven to expand to gain more power.

This was the case with Bernie Madoff and his now famous Ponzi scheme. As he became more powerful, he wanted more. Did he really need all that money? His scheme was estimated at roughly $65 billion. His identity needed this appearance of continuing success as he established a lifestyle and connections with powerful people. It is easy to see how this energy can run wild and take over your life. In the end, Madoff showed little to no remorse and even made a statement criticizing his investors and calling them greedy.

A person with a powerful negative ego-identity lacks compassion, caring and the ability to accept responsibility or apologize for hurting others. The more you identify with your ego-identity, the more disconnected you are from spirit. How important is maintaining your identity to you? Take a moment and answer this question honestly. You may be surprised at what you uncover about yourself.

How Your Ego-Identity was Created

Creating an ego-identity is like emptying your kitchen and making an elaborate soup. You add hundreds of ingredients, start stirring … and hope it tastes good. Your identity was created the same way.

Your Identity Recipe

- Start with your parents' DNA & traits (physical & emotional)
- Add some of their beliefs about what is right and wrong
- Add a shot of guilt and shame
- Don't forget a strong dose of fear
- Hopefully some praise and encouragement
- A pinch of undeserving and unworthiness
- Add some outside-the-home experiences, influences and some religion
- Sprinkle in a few key people who had influence on your thinking

Stir this all together and you have the recipe for your identity. There are parts of it you will like and parts you will hate. In the end, your identity is not good and it is not bad. It simply is.

Your identity is also tied to your energy and what you attract. You are continually attracting people and situations based on this identity.

In addition, your identity serves as a filter. It allows certain people and situations in and keeps others away. I like to think of my ego-identity as the bark of a tree. A tree needs the bark to remain protected and to survive. The bark is malleable which allows certain elements to enter. It also protects the tree and blocks harmful elements. At a high level, this bark, or identity, only allows positive elements in and blocks negative ones. A positive ego-identity will develop as you move away from the negative ego and the desire to maintain a false identity.

The more you let go of the importance of your identity, the more powerful you become. Your goal is to simply be yourself all the time and not worry about the outside world or your image. Then you become free from the fear of having to be something or someone. This is difficult to achieve because the negative ego is always attempting to pull you in and disconnect you from source energy.

Be aware of your desires and actions. Are you doing something for yourself or to feed the identity? Ask yourself this question all day long. It will help you see when you are slipping into a negative space.

Many, if not all, of your actions are designed to maintain the ego-identity you have created. Remember, you are fighting to keep this identity alive at all costs. This is not a conscious action. You are subconsciously trapped in a loop based on maintaining who you believe you are right now. As you let go of this false identity, your desire to maintain the illusion will dissolve. Most of your identity is tied to how you received attention and love. This is based on deep conditioning from your childhood.

The big question is simple – when did you receive attention and love from your parents? What did you have to do to get their attention? When were they nice to you? When did they make you feel accepted?

These feelings are based on what you learned growing up and how your parents responded to you. One of my friends, Jim, always talked about how he received positive attention when he did everything his father asked of him right away. His brother, Mike, received negative attention because he did not respond as quickly. Mike was often criticized by his parents.

Your first reaction might be "that's great for Jim. He received a lot of positive feedback." Yes and no. In this world, every feeling and action is two-sided. We call it the yin and yang. A positive and negative charge of energy is always present. Jim *did* receive positive feedback and it became a part of his identity. As an adult, he felt compelled to help everyone, even at his own expense. This is how he was conditioned to receive positive feedback and love. His identity was that he was the reliable and dependable one. He only received positive attention when he did what everyone else wanted.

However, to break this identity he is going to have become selfish and risk losing the love he received for such behavior. This fear paralyzes people and keeps them trapped in their ego-identity. This is how Jim was conditioned to receive love. How will he receive love if he gives up this behavior? This fear paralyzes people and holds them in the ego-identity.

Mike was the opposite. He received attention for not doing what his father desired. On the positive side, Mike was more independent and focused on his desires. He was able to say no and was not manipulated as easily as Jim.

The negative side results from *how* Mike received attention. To a child, negative attention is better than no attention. He had been conditioned to receive attention and gain power through conflict and defiance. Consequently he constantly argued and created conflict in all areas of his life to receive attention. This became his identity.

As you examine yourself, you will uncover many similar traits as you expose your own identity. There will be pieces of it you like and want to keep, and other parts you want to dissolve.

Your identity is tied to your karmic mission. You chose this identity to help you move though the emotional issues you are here to experience. Do not judge yourself or others. Each person has the perfect identity for the work they came here to complete. Accept this fact and appreciate yourself for who you are in this lifetime.

Dissolving Your Negative Ego-Identity

As mentioned earlier, you need an identity to play here on earth. Moving forward and busting your karma will require you to dissolve the negative part of your ego. This is challenging because you are actually giving up a piece of yourself. It does not matter if the traits and feelings are positive or negative. You are very comfortable with who you are right now. Giving up even a small piece of your identity is very scary.

The reason you are so terrified to change is fear of the unknown. As you transition to a higher level of energy and break your karmic cycle, it is no longer necessary to hold onto your old identity. I know this sounds great, but your negative ego will put up a fight before it goes. The natural tendency for human beings is to slide back into familiar patterns. How many times have you recycled an old relationship or brought a negative friend back into your life? This is the result of fear and a resistance to change.

Dissolving your negative ego-identity means you are changing who you are on a deep emotional level. You will begin to vibrate at a different level of energy. In this new vibration, you are going to attract different people and situations.

In chapter two I gave an example of approval-seeking energy. In approval-seeking energy you will attract people who make you feel like you are not good enough. These people may still be in your life. As your energy shifts, and you are no longer seeking approval, there is no need for this type of energy. The friends you attracted at that time are no longer necessary. I know that may sound a bit harsh but I want you to see this from the perspective of energy. Your new energy no longer desires these people and knows they are not good for you.

"But Joe, these have been my friends for many years. Are you telling me to cut them out of my life?"

No, but you will have a different feeling about them and they will have a different feeling about you. It is not necessary to do anything dramatic. Eventually you will naturally drift apart unless they are also working on moving to a higher level.

In the early stages of this karma busting work, you may feel disconnected and have a strong desire to distance yourself from others. Your soul requires space to make these transitions and to heal itself. You may also feel lost and confused for a while. You are used to being a certain person and now you have to adjust to being a whole new you.

I worked with a woman named Jane who always felt tremendous guilt if she was not taking care of everyone in her family. She had always received positive attention growing up when she was doing things for others. The minute we started working together, I told her she had to start putting her needs first. That meant Jane had to focus on her own desires before those of anyone else. This created deep feelings of guilt for Jane. She felt terrible making plans for herself and not taking care of her family. In her eyes she would become a terrible person by prioritizing her needs. Being the caretaker was her entire identity. She did not know how to put her needs first.

Busting your identity requires that you to push yourself into a completely different place. You will be extremely uncomfortable. The big issue is learning to receive love and attention in a completely different way.

In this case, Jane is now loving and honoring herself. She has learned to receive love from others in this new position. Initially this brought up much fear because Jane was not sure she would receive love in her new identity. It takes time, commitment and discipline to truly dissolve your negative ego-identity.

Who Are You ... Really?

It is time to move into your deepest truth. Who are you?

Three Levels of Identity

1. **The surface you:** The person you show the world
2. **The ego-identity you:** The person you were trained and conditioned to be
3. **Your true spirit-self**

Your current identity is based on your level of awareness and attachment to the false identity you absorbed as a child. As your awareness heightens, the attachment to the identity weakens. You realize and accept that it is not necessary to hold onto your old identity. It does not serve you in your higher state of energy and awareness. Remain aware of the three states of identity and it will be very easy to see where you are at a given time.

Monitoring Yourself

It is important to catch yourself as you begin to drift into negative ego-identity. As human beings, we must remain very aware and vigilant of these tendencies. The negative ego is insidious and always looking for an opportunity to pull you back in.

Signs you are slipping:

- The desire to be right
- Negative judgment
- Showing off
- Ridiculing others
- Bad mouthing others
- Using your will to force others to do what you desire
- Not accepting the desires of others
- Forcing your ideas and concepts
- Blaming others

The more aware you are, the easier it will be to catch yourself and make an adjustment. The desire to be right along with negative judgments are usually the most common problem-creators. Energy builds momentum as you hold focus. You may be arguing with someone and feel you are right. As you hold this energy and press to make your point, you are building momentum. The further you go, the harder it is to pull back and adjust. The negative ego feeds off the energy you are creating as you battle to make your point.

In most of these cases, an argument ensues and both people walk away feeling upset. I know what you are thinking … *"am I suppose to be a pushover and let everyone take advantage of me?"* How the situation plays out is all based on perspective. Having to be right is the negative ego's best friend.

Having to be right occurs in a multitude of circumstances throughout the day. Sometimes you may tell your child he or she cannot do something. As a parent, it is your job to protect and guide – even when your child (especially a teenager) does not agree. This is not a right or wrong scenario. It is not even a 'having to be right' scenario. Here you are making the decision you feel is best for your child and holding your ground as a parent.

Work and business situations present many opportunities for conflict. You have to be passionate about your ideas. However, try to be open to the ideas of others. Even if you do not agree with what they say, you can listen and decide which ideas are most beneficial without creating conflict.

Then, we have my favorite – dealing with family … particularly parents and siblings. A lot of conflict is generated in families because each person is still defending their identity and position within the family structure. Family members will generate our greatest challenges. This makes perfect sense because it is this karma you are here to break.

Your family conflicts provide powerful learning lessons. Put your ego aside and see the situation from a higher place. Step out of the situation and become an observer. Look for the emotion and energy that needs to be cleared, instead of jumping into an argument and creating conflict.

My family – they are Italian – and they like to use guilt as a manipulative tool. Guilt is, of course, one of the most powerful emotional tools. Not being available for a family function was unacceptable to my family. Instead of honoring my time, I was made to feel I was doing something wrong. This moved me into a defensive posture. I felt I was right in having other plans and defended my position. This caused a conflict and a power struggle ensued. In the old days, I always gave in to the feelings of guilt and shame. I would cancel my plans to make everyone else happy. My rationale was simple. I was doing the best thing for the family, even if it was the worst thing for myself.

In reality, I was falling back into my old identity and old patterns for receiving love (albeit distorted love). When I did what my family wanted me to do, even at my own expense, I received positive energy. They were happy, but I was conflicted. On some level, I knew there was something very wrong with this picture.

As I became more powerful and started to dissolve my ego-identity, things began to change. I was then able to miss the family event, deal with the guilt and hold my position. I no longer required approval from my family. In my distorted view, the feeling of acceptance I received when I canceled my plans was love. The truth is, it was nothing more than pure manipulation by people who only cared about themselves. If they really loved me, they would have accepted the fact that I was unavailable and honored my decision.

This was a life-changing revelation for me. It was a difficult idea to accept but it was true. Those who truly love you love you all the time. That is the definition of unconditional love. Everything else is conditional love and is based on the desire to control.

The next time you find yourself feeling defensive, know you are not being loved. Instead of defending yourself, move into your true feelings at the moment. When my family did not accept the fact I had plans, my first reaction was anger, a surface emotion as discussed earlier. As I went deeper, I realized I was hurt and felt disrespected and unimportant. Whenever I gave in, I did not allow myself to move deeper and feel my true emotions.

As your ego-identity is being dissolved, prepare yourself for many of these episodes and some emotional turbulence. Your old identity is filled with emotional energy that must be addressed. The truth about who you think you are and how others have made you feel is extremely powerful.

Moving into your truth will be challenging. You will realize that much of what you believed to be true is not. This shatters your belief system and begins to break down your false identity. The more you remain honest with your feelings, the easier it will be to let go of the old and move into your new spirit-self. The real you is filled with love and acceptance. Busting your karma allows you to reconnect with your true self and feel the love you are here to experience.

5 Your Good and Bad List

When were you good and when were you bad?

As a child, you were made to feel you were good or bad in different situations. These feelings and beliefs are still with you today. Defining these feelings and the behavior that drives them is critical to busting your karma.

There is no such thing as good and bad in the world of energy, but it sure does exist here on earth. The majority of our decisions and reactions are based on what we deem to be right and wrong or good and bad. We learned these lessons as children. These lessons are a direct result of the reactions we received in various situations.

Here is an example of how this happens.

A little girl, Molly, asks her father for money to buy ice cream. He replies, "No, that is a waste of money." This same episode plays out a number of times until Molly realizes she is not to ask for anything. The negative response makes her believe she is bad for asking for what she desires. "Dad does not love me when I ask for something. He loves me when I do things for him and expect nothing in return." This creates a powerful association when Molly asks for things she wants. Now Molly feels she is bad when asking for what she wants..

Molly came to me to work on the karma of feeling undeserving and unworthy. She held the energy and belief that asking for what she wanted made her bad. So, for Molly, asking was bad; not asking was good. And we all want to be good. This feeling is now deeply rooted in Molly's energy, beliefs and DNA. Molly's desire is to be liked, accepted and good. To achieve this goal, she must deny herself and not ask for anything. She has been systematically trained this way.

Once these deep feelings and beliefs are engrained, it is very difficult to let them go. This also becomes a piece of your ego-identity that was addressed in the previous chapter. Now you have to uncover your original beliefs and feelings to stop the negative behavior and break the energy pattern.

Like most of this work, it is simple yet challenging. We all want to be liked, which means to be good, to receive positive feedback. Once we are trapped in this approval seeking cycle, it is challenging to get out.

Time to Create Your List

Children know what works and what does not work. They act and react based on the feelings and energy received from their parents. Once they realize what they need to do to receive attention, they continue to take that action. This is how our core patterns develop and how our brains become hardwired.

Now it is time for you to uncover your own truth about when you were good and bad as a child. This truth will explain a lot about your current behavior and decision-making process.

Grab a pad of paper and pen and make your list.

When were you good?

Examples: "*When I did my chores, received good grades, listened to my father, was reliable and responsible,*" *etc.*

What you did to be good	How you were made to feel

When were you bad?

Examples: "*When I asked for something, did not listen, received poor grades, questioned my mother and father,*" etc.

What you did to be bad	How you were made to feel

As you review your two lists, some things will become clear to you. Observe how your reactions and beliefs are tied to your good and bad list. Are you still following these same patterns trying to be good to receive approval?

What happened when you were bad?

How did you feel?

How did others make you feel?

How did you react to the negative energy coming at you?

Did you feel guilt and shame? Maybe you felt anger or disgust?

Becoming aware of all of these feelings and reactions will be a great asset as you move forward.

The driving desire for all human beings is to feel loved by their parents. We will do whatever it takes to receive even the slightest hint of love. If you never felt loved by your mother or father, it is not likely to happen now no matter what you do. On a logical level you realize this, but your subconscious desire to be loved is so powerful that you cannot stop trying.

Every person I have worked with, regardless of age, race or background – all believed things would change. They held the belief that sooner or later Mom and Dad would love and appreciate them for who they are if they did everything "right." Most people expend tremendous amounts of energy trying to be good to receive this long sought after approval. When it does not happen, the results are emotionally devastating. This will be played out with family, friends and at work.

You must accept the fact that you may never receive the love from them that you desire and deal with the sadness attached to this truth.

Now you are a karma buster and the world is about to change!

You are going to move in to a new world and become a ***Bad Ass…in a good way.***

Busting karma requires you to be "bad" based on your current beliefs. You are not really being bad but you think you are, which creates the same feeling. Moving past this feeling is a challenging part of the process. Don't worry. In time you will become comfortable with your new identity.

6 Your Karmic Map and Chakra Energy System

The karmic map is your blueprint based on the emotional work you are here to experience. Imagine you made a list of the emotions you wanted to feel before you arrived here on earth. These emotions are then tied to your parents and DNA. These feelings are held in your Chakra Energy System. This system holds your energy and creates your unique vibration of energy. Your vibration attracts situations and people into your life. When you break your karma, you shift the energy of your Chakra System. By doing this, you change your DNA and create different outcomes in your life.

The Chakra Energy System

Chakra is a Sanskrit (ancient Indian) word that means spiral or wheel. Chakras are energy points in your body, running from the crown of your head to the base of your spine. All of your feelings and beliefs are held as energy in your Chakra System. This energy creates vibration that goes out into the universe. Your life is a reflection of the energy you hold internally.

You may feel different sensations in specific parts of your body at certain times. These are issues connected to a specific chakra. I was working with a client, Tom, who had to make a speech to a new division of his company. A week before the speech, his throat began to close up. We had to work on the feeling that was causing this issue. As we went deeper, Tom remembered an episode in second grade. He was reading aloud in front of the class and began to stutter. The teacher berated him in front of his peers. He felt humiliated and ashamed. He remembered having the same feeling in his throat that day.

This was one of those anchoring feelings I mentioned earlier. Tom identified the feeling as a fear of being embarrassed in front of his peers at work this time – but it was the same exact feeling he had experienced almost thirty years earlier. We cleared the energy and his throat was fine. He delivered the presentation without incident.

You do not have to be an expert with chakras to move forward with the karma buster process, but I wanted you to understand how chakras work with regard to your energy. If you are interested in learning more about chakras, I would suggest the book by my mentor and spiritual advisor Susan Kerr entitled *The System for Soul Memory.* It is by far the most comprehensive and detailed book I have read on the subject.

These are the Chaka points in your body. You will notice an eighth chakra, Moon Center. This is a very powerful chakra in the nose and mouth area. It relates to feelings of responsibility in your life and how you feel about being responsible for yourself and others.

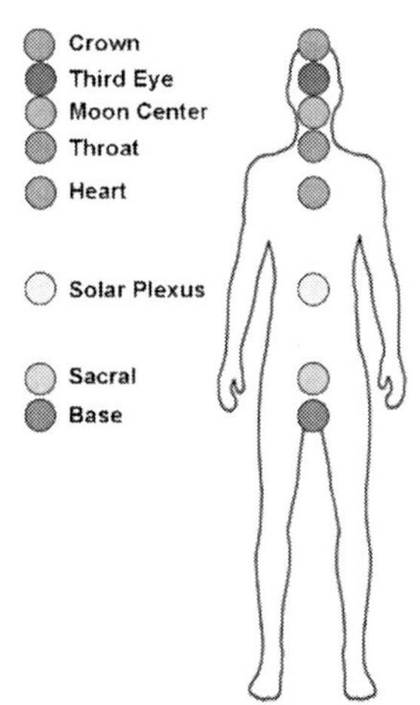

Body Position of Chakras

Crown: Crown of your head

Third Eye: Forehead

Moon Center: Nose and mouth

Throat

Heart: Center of chest

Solar Plexus: Abdominal area

Sacral: Pelvic area

Base or Root: Base of your spine

Chakra Energy System Development

Your chakras develop from the bottom up, base to crown. The moment you are conceived, you begin to absorb energy from your environment. Knowing your family situation, you can easily imagine the feelings in your home before you arrived. What type of energy do you feel you were absorbing before you were born? If there was a lot of tension and discord, you began absorbing those feelings.

The Chakra System develops from conception to age eight. All your current issues are anchored in unresolved feelings from the first eight years of life. Each chakra holds different feelings and relates to specific issues.

The following is a quick snapshot with the age associated with development:

Base (0-1): This is the anchor and holds feelings about safety, success and being loved. Issues about money and protection live here. Many people have lower back pain based on feelings in this area.

Sacral (1-2): Located in the pelvic area, this chakra relates to relationships and trust. People may have sexual dysfunction and women may have issues with reproductive organs.

Solar Plexus (2-3): This is the stomach area where we hold anger. This is the reason so many people have digestive issues and ulcers. It is also the power center to hold your chi, your energy.

Heart (3-4): Your ability to share and receive love is held here. If you have trouble expressing yourself or receiving love, your heart chakra is blocked.

Throat (4-5): This chakra is the area where the communication ability is based. If you are not being heard or if you struggle to find your voice, this is the area to investigate.

Moon Center (5-6): This is where you took your first breath and it relates to your sense of responsibility for yourself and others. This is a very powerful chakra to recognize as you break your karma.

Third Eye (6-7): This is your psychic area. When you have a feeling or premonition, it is your Third Eye at work. The more you trust your feelings, the better your psychic abilities will become.

Crown (7-8): You receive your energy from this chakra. The more open you are, the easier the energy will flow. Judgment often blocks this flow of energy.

As you become more aware and connected to your feelings, you will feel things in certain parts of your body. You will be able to connect the feeling to certain chakras and understand where the feeling originated.

7 Do You Really Have a Destiny?

There are many beliefs about destiny based on an individual's upbringing and religious background. Some people believe destiny is set in stone, while others see many possible outcomes.

I will offer my view based on my research and personal experiences. I believe everyone comes to earth with specific emotional work to complete. Your karmic map comes to you in the form of desires. When you have a strong desire to do something, it is your karma (what you came here to do) creating the emotion.

You will be faced with many opportunities in life. Each of these opportunities requires a decision. This is where the wild card of free will comes into play. You have the ability to step into the unknown and expand yourself, or pull back and move into fear. Each situation creates an opportunity for growth. The universe will give you many opportunities to be courageous and grow.

Busting your karma requires you to step into the unknown. This creates extreme discomfort, a feeling we usually try to avoid. Not only are we uncomfortable because of this change, but we also have to deal with the opinions and beliefs of family and friends.

Let me give you an example of how this may play out. Your destiny and karma are linked together as part of your map. You will have desires and then you will have to decide whether or not to act on these desires.

Let's say you came here to become an artist. In this case, art and creativity will come easy to you. There is a strong feeling or desire to pursue this path.

Your family is very conservative and fear-based. They know you are talented but they are fearful that you will not be able to make a living as an artist. The fear drives them to insist you go to school and learn a safer skill. This is where free will and the decision-making process come into play. Will you follow your desire or be influenced by the fear being placed upon you? Remember, we also have the desire to make our parents happy and proud.

What are you going to do?

I like to call this a *Crossroads Moment*. There will be many of these opportunities as you move through your life. You will have to decide what to do. Each decision moves you closer to your true destiny or further away. Your feelings will tell you the best decision for you at that time. There will be feelings of love and fear. However, there is one type of fear that can be particularly confusing.

Let's continue with the example of the artist. You have created a situation with two options. There is the safe decision to become an accountant or the riskier one where you go to art school. Your family wants you to pursue accounting. What are you feeling as you think about making this decision? Part of you wants your parents' approval, but deep down you want to be an artist. There are feelings of fear, but these fears are of the unknown – not about actually becoming an artist. This is a huge distinction to make when evaluating fears.

We all have fear of the unknown. In this case, you do not have fear of becoming an artist. The feeling attached to the artistic path is love. You do not have the feeling of love attached to being an accountant. You have the fear of disapproval from your family. At your core you are driven to follow your desire to become an artist. Now you have a decision to make. What will you do? In most cases, you will follow the path of least resistance and become an accountant to make your parents happy. No worries. You can always decide to become an artist later.

When I left high school, my first job was driving a truck, delivering beer, in Brooklyn, N.Y. I liked being outside, and there was a sense of freedom in my job. As soon as we finished our route, we brought the truck back and went home. If we pushed ourselves a little, we could be back early and have the rest of the day off.

My uncle worked at a bank. He told my mother he could get me a job there. This was a good way to start a real career in banking. I agreed and went to work in a check processing center. I sat in a chair and processed checks as they moved through a conveyor belt. On the second day, I went to my car to drive home and I was shaking. I hated being in there all day. The next day I went to my boss and told him I was quitting. What a relief. That was certainly not my destiny.

You will have strong feelings like this throughout your life. The question is will you follow your desires or listen to others and be practical? These decisions are all about feelings. You make a decision and then you feel a feeling. Are you happy or sad? Are you excited or depressed? These are the issues and feelings you will experience along your life path.

Crossroads Exercise

This is a great exercise to help you evaluate how you have been making decisions up to this point in your life. Be honest and be sure to feel the emotions attached to each decision.

Step 1: Make a list of the major decisions you have made in your life. These include things like selecting a school, getting engaged, accepting or rejecting a job offer, marriage, having kids, moving, making a major purchase, buying a house and so on.

Example: *Decided to attend school A.*

Step 2: Answer these questions…

- Why did you make that decision?
- Who was influencing you at the time?
- How did you feel about the decision?
- What was the outcome?

Step 3: Get into the feelings…

- How did you feel as you made the decision?

  This is important so I want you to revisit the situation and remember what you were feeling at the time. Make a list of all the feelings that come up for you.

Step 4: Evaluate…

- How do you feel about your decision now? It doesn't matter how it turned out. Focus on your feelings. You may have taken a risk that did not work out but you still feel it was the best decision for you at the time. This is not about the results – it is about your feelings. In many cases, decisions that seem to go wrong are the most important to our growth.

What This Exercise is Telling You

As you examine your list, you will see patterns emerging. Have you been taking risks, going against the majority and expanding yourself? Maybe you realize you followed the safe path to keep everyone else happy. How does this make you feel? Do you want to continue along this path or is it time for a change?

When you do this correctly, you are sure to feel a surge of emotions. Allow those feelings to flow through you. Again, there is no judgment involved. Do not go back and beat yourself up. Feel the feelings of each event. That is where the true wisdom lies. When you feel the pain and joy of these decisions, you are tapping into the wisdom of the universe. You now understand the experience on an emotional level. This is true wisdom.

This exercise will also help you have more compassion for others and make you less judgmental. You will see how others have struggled in much the same way with their decisions and issues.

As you move forward, stay in touch with how you feel *before* making a decision. What is driving your process? How do you really feel? What are your desires? How will you feel when you do what is best for yourself? Be ready to feel selfish. This feeling will come up a lot as you begin to follow your path and do what is best for yourself.

Making Your Big Plays

You will also have opportunities and desires to make big changes in your life. I like to call these your *Big Plays.* These are the decisions that have the greatest impact on your life. Most of these situations will come to you in the form of opportunities or desires.

We will look at opportunities first. These are situations you have created based on your desires. Sometimes you are faced with a life-changing decision. When I use the term "life-changing," I mean situations relative to your life and your comfort with *change.*

One of my clients, James, is a very conservative guy. He works locally and values his family time. James loves the fact that he is home for dinner most evenings and is always around on the weekend for his kids' activities. One day, his boss calls him in with an opportunity for a significant promotion. The only caveat is that the position requires him to travel about 50% of the time.

This presented a big dilemma for James. He would receive a significant increase in salary and status, but he would have to spend more time away from his family. James discusses the offer with his wife and she feels it is too good to pass up. In addition, if he turns it down, his career might stall and he might not be considered for other promotions.

This may sound like a very easy decision to you. It was not the case for James, as he reflected on the travel involved. I brought him into his feelings and he said he was feeling a lot of guilt. The key was finding out where the guilt was originating in his past. Remember, all of these feelings are linked to an unresolved issue in your past.

There are tens of thousands of people who would not have given this decision a second thought. On paper this is a no-brainer. Not to James. Going deeper, James linked this back to his own father who was always working and never home. His father did not travel but he was away nonetheless.

"I do not want to be like my father," James exclaimed. We moved though the guilt and anger James was holding onto about his father. As he released the energy, he realized he could travel and still remain close with his family. He had to resolve the feeling of guilt and accept the fear of repeating his father's behavior. As these issues were addressed, James was able to move forward and accept the promotion. This was a life-changing decision for James and his career has flourished as a result. His family life has changed, but he is balancing his new responsibility very well.

Desire is different in the sense that you have a feeling without the opportunity being presented to you. Desires are more challenging because you cannot see what is ahead of you as you can in James' situation. You just feel something and know it is the direction to move in, even though there are no visible signs.

This happens a lot with actors, entrepreneurs and inventors. There is no logic as to what causes their desire. There is only a feeling, an instinct, a deep desire. I remember reading about the actress Hillary Swank. After her parents separated, she expressed her desire to act. Her mother supported her desire by leaving their home in Washington State and heading to Los Angeles with little money, experience or contacts. They reportedly lived in their car until her mother saved enough money for a small apartment. In this case, Hillary was fortunate to have the support of her mother.

Sometimes we are not so lucky. I have heard countless stories of family discord when a new desire is expressed. In one case, a third generation Ivy League attorney suddenly decided he was being 'called' to become a veterinarian. His father disowned him and he was removed from the will. The attorney went on to become a successful veterinarian. Years later he made peace with his father, but he said their relationship was never the same.

When you have support along with your desire, your path will be easier, although it will still be challenging. Without support, you have to overcome many feelings and emotions and display great courage to move forward. You will feel guilt, uncertainty, mistrust, fear and anger with those who will not support you. These experiences will also disclose the people who truly love you. When you are courageous and follow your desires, you expose the fears of others. They usually do not like that and may react strongly. On some level, you are actually helping them uncover some of their issues. They may choose to ignore these feelings or deal with them. This is not your issue. It is for them to resolve on their own.

My family recently experienced a Big Play when we moved from New York, where we have all lived our entire lives, to southern California. My wife and I are both from Italian families. Their idea of moving away is moving to the next zip code area. Our Big Play was met with shock and opposition by some family members. We did not have a great opportunity waiting for us. In their eyes, this was an act of insanity. The only reason we wanted to move was because our son decided he wanted to go to college in California.

This was a major karma buster move for us. We had to deal with the guilt of moving away from our families. It was a big deal for us to leave the Italian culture we grew up with in New York. We were raised to believe you are supposed to be present to support your family at all times. Now we were heading to the golden coast to follow our own desires. Once again, change all depends on your perspective and belief system. I have dozens of friends and acquaintances who have lived all over the world – and never thought twice about moving.

The Big Play is going to be different for each person based on your feelings, emotions and beliefs. No Big Play is better or worse, easier or more difficult. It is all relative, based on your unique emotions.

Becoming a karma buster requires you to follow your desires – be courageous. Have fun!

What About Your Destiny?

You may have the destiny to become a great artist. If you are unable to follow your true path, your mission will be incomplete. In the event you don't become an artist, you have still moved though a lot of the karma, emotions and feelings you came here to experience. You may have felt regret, failure and intense disappointment this time around. No worries. You will have the opportunity to come back and try again.

Don't worry about your destiny. All you have to do is follow your feelings and trust your instincts. The more you do this, the easier your life will become. One of our greatest challenges is trust. Do you believe the universe will support you regardless of what is happening in your life?

It is very difficult to have faith and trust when your life seems to be a big mess. Years ago I had a session with a trance medium in New York City. As the name implies, a trance medium goes into a trance and connects with beings from the other side. This seemed really weird to me initially, but I was in my exploring stage and was open to new experiences.

The trance medium's name is Bob Johnson and he is a truly amazing guy. He is an older man, in his seventies, with an angelic face. My wife likened him to Santa Claus. At the time of our session, I was really struggling and my faith was being tested. I was questioning all of these processes, God, my teachers, everyone I knew and everything I was doing. If I was here to do this work and I was following my path, why was it so difficult? Why was I struggling to make a living? Why didn't people call me for sessions and speaking engagements? Why did I seem to be running into so many obstacles? These were some of the questions I posed to Bob in his trance state.

He smiled at me with a devilish look and said, "You must have these experiences to master the work you are here to do." He continued, "How can you help others without experiencing all of the emotions and feelings they are experiencing?" These comments moved me into a very different feeling. What I was experiencing was preparing me for the work I was here to do. It was getting me ready for the karma I was here to clear.

Then he said, "Have faith, Joe. You can only see a small piece of your life. The universe sees your entire life and is always guiding you for your highest good ... have faith in the big picture." This has been a very challenging lesson for me. As a New Yorker with a focus on results, the idea of waiting and trusting is not exactly the way I am used to living.

The universe is always sending us messages if we are willing to pay attention. I seem to receive a lot of messages through movies and music. A few weeks after my session with Bob, I went to see the movie *Cinderella Man* starring Russell Crowe. This is the true story of a boxer named James J. Braddock from New Jersey. He was an up-and-coming fighter in the late 1920s. In 1929, he gets a shot at the light heavyweight title and loses. His life takes a turn for the worse after the fight, as the country moves into The Great Depression.

Braddock's status is diminished and he finds himself fighting in small clubs for very little money. He loses most of his fights and takes a beating in the process. Finally he breaks his right hand and is stripped of his boxing license. His financial situation is bleak and his boxing career is over. He goes to the government relief office for help, and is so desperate, he even begs the boxing promoters he knows for money to pay his electric bills.

To support his family, he walks miles to the docks in New Jersey and works unloading cargo ships. Because his right hand is broken, he is forced to use his left. As a fighter, Braddock was known for his powerful right hand and weak left hand. He was also criticized for his plodding style and poor footwork.

A year or so later, in 1934, his manager appears out of nowhere with an offer for a fight. He can fight at Madison Square Garden in New York City in a preliminary bout before the heavyweight championship fight! The boxer scheduled to fight is injured and no one else would take the bout against the number one heavyweight contender without time to train.

Braddock is excited and the $250 purse will relieve his financial situation for a while.

Braddock is supposed to be a sacrificial lamb with virtually no chance of winning. He is there to make a decent showing and collect his money. As the fight begins, Braddock is under siege by his stronger and younger opponent. He is knocked down in the first round and seems to be headed for an early exit. Suddenly he rises and proceeds to pump two powerful left-handed jabs into the face of his opponent.

In the third round the impossible happens as Braddock scores a knock out. After the fight, his manager says, "Where in the world did that left hand come from … and since when could you move like that?" Braddock explained how he had to use his left hand on the docks after he broke his right, and how the long walks to the docks strengthened his legs. Little did he expect that these challenges and hardships were getting him ready for a future he could never have imagined.

A year later, Braddock, as the biggest underdog of all time, shocked the world by winning the heavyweight championship. During his years of struggle, I wonder if Jim Braddock ever thought, "No worries. This is preparing me for the biggest moment of my life."

I think not.

I remember walking out the theatre thinking, "*oh, that universe sure knows how to send a message.*"

It is easy to have faith when everything is going well. True faith is knowing that everything is happening for your highest good all the time, even when there are no apparent signs of positive change. A lot of trust is required to live this way. This continues to be an ongoing lesson for me … living with the knowledge and trust that the universe is always looking out for us.

Look for signs and validation in the world around you. There are always signs available to help you if you are open and aware. These signs may come from the strangest places, but believe me, they are always present if you know where to look. Be aware and ask for help when you pray and meditate.

The universe has never let me down when I have asked for help.

8 Maintaining Your Karma Busting Ways Daily

Knowing and experiencing these processes is wonderful. Your awareness is heightened, you are less judgmental, there is more clarity and you feel empowered. The key to success is maintaining your karma busting ways all the time.

I frequently use the analogy of physical fitness. If your desire is to lose weight and get into shape, you would create a plan to achieve your goal. You would deal with some karma and the emotional issues related to your weight. Then you would begin to exercise and modify your diet. After months, or even years, of work, dedication and discipline, you reach your mark. Now what? Would you suddenly stop doing everything that got you to this point?

Maintaining your new physique requires the same level of commitment and discipline. You would not abandon all of the positive emotional and lifestyle changes you made and start eating donuts three meals a day.

Your karma busting work is no different.

It is very important to maintain discipline. You have to keep on meditating and clearing negative energy as it comes up. Be aware of judgments and feelings at all times. This will keep you sharp and engaged. There are many people who make great progress and suddenly drift away. They begin to slide back into their old energy and self-destructive behavior. Remember, the dark side is always waiting to pull you back in at a weak moment.

We frequently see this with weight loss. How many people have you seen lose a lot of weight, only to gain it all back … and more.

What happened?

In most cases they were not doing the emotional work necessary to hold the energy level required to maintain their newfound success. This happens in all areas of life including career, money, health and relationships.

Because you are doing the emotional work, you are better prepared to maintain positive changes. You are better prepared, but you are still vulnerable – especially when facing a stressful situation or major change in your life.

The negative ego is just sitting patiently, waiting for you to get full of yourself. Then it will strike like a cobra – without warning – and send you into a downward spiral.

Your greatest asset with regard to this work is humility. Love yourself and know that you are amazing. You have shown great courage and dedication to reach this point. This is about self love, not feeling you are better than everyone else who may not be as far along the path.

Be consistent and stay on your game.

Giving Yourself a Break

Working on your energy at this level of emotion is challenging. It is impossible to maintain 100% focus all the time. It is for that reason you must be very nice to yourself.

What does this mean?

It means you need to honor how you feel.

You may need to take a break from meditating for a while. Maybe a few days or more will help rejuvenate yourself. If you feel tired or emotionally drained, be sure to rest. Take a nap, walk the dog, sit in the park or just zone out in front of the TV. Another great thing is connecting to nature. Stay grounded and connected to source energy.

A lot of people struggle with the idea of nurturing themselves. It brings up feelings of guilt and shame. This is also based on what you learned as a child. How did your family react when you said you were tired or distressed? Were you honored or ridiculed? Was there support or scorn?

As you continue to love yourself, there will be a desire to honor your feelings. You may feel some guilt and shame at first but, in time, you will feel comfortable nurturing yourself. This is all part of the process and it will help you as you begin to create your life in a new way.

9 Creating Your Life in a Whole New Way

As you bust the old karma, there is no longer a desire to recreate your life based on the feelings and beliefs of the past. Although this may sound exciting, it can be also be scary. In the old karma, you were on a wheel and knew what to expect. Now you are in new territory. You do not know what is coming.

Let's say you broke karma in the relationship area. The old cycle was always the same. You met someone, went out for a while and then he or she cheated on you. First you felt helpless, unwanted and betrayed. Then you were able to feel like a victim and complain to everyone. You were right again (your ego loved it) and the wheel was complete.

This time, because you busted the old karma, the person you met is wonderful and makes you feel loved. Although you always wanted this feeling, it is new and very scary. You freak out because this has never happened to you. You do not know what to do because you are expecting this person to cheat on you, but instead this person keeps on loving you.

Dealing with this new life is going to be challenging, especially in the beginning of the transformation. You must be prepared to move into new feelings. Knowing the challenges that lie ahead will make the transition much easier.

You are no longer creating your life based on old beliefs and feelings. There is no map to follow or outcome to expect. In the past, you were following your old Karmic Wheel around and around. Now you are off the wheel. You are creating new outcomes … and the possibilities are endless.

This moves you from unconscious creation to conscious creation. What is the big difference between the two? In your old karma you were recreating situations over and over again by recycling the same energy. You were not aware of these cycles because your energy level was too low. You were unable to see what you were doing.

Now you are aware, or as Buddha said, "Now I am awake." At your higher level of awareness and energy, you have the ability to create what you desire. This does not mean you will begin to create exactly what you want at all times. The difference is you now know and accept the fact that you can create it.

When you create something unpleasant, you know there is an unresolved feeling and belief that must be cleared. Clearing it will be, believe it or not, the easy part. Unpleasant creations are easy because you have seen this story before and know how to manage it. You know how to be fat, but you do not know how to be fit.

Look at your most challenging issues and you will see how they continue to resurface – even after you work though all the feelings and karma. This happens because you are so familiar with the feeling. This is your comfort zone … the place you know so well and feel most comfortable living.

The issue may be loneliness, sickness, money, relationship drama or weight. The more aware you are the better. You will begin to see these episodes coming and eventually there will no longer be a desire to continue repeating the same old story. You will stop recreating the past and begin to consciously create what you desire.

Now the Fun Begins

Creating positive outcomes will be more challenging than you think. Once again, this makes no logical sense to most people. Once you are aware, you may think, "all I have to do is focus to create what I really want."

Well … yes and no.

As you move into conscious creation, you will have to deal with the other side of the rainbow. I know what you are thinking … *"what does that mean, Joe?"*

That means you have to feel all the feelings on the opposite side of your issue.

I like to use actors or musicians as examples because they have very specific desires and most do not deal with success very well. I worked in New York bars and nightclubs for many years. I used to make a joke that I was the only person working there who was not an aspiring actor, musician or model. If you asked any of these people what they desired, the answer was always the same. "I want to be rich and famous working as a ______________." Fill in the occupational blank.

Then it happens. You're an actor/actress and all of a sudden you are plucked from obscurity and you get your big break. One day you can't pay your rent and the next day you can't leave your apartment because of the publicity. You have money, fame, opportunity ... all the things you have always desired.

Now what? Unfortunately there is a long list of very famous and successful people who have not fared very well. We have seen it all ... from drug abuse to suicide.

This, of course, begs the next question. "If I received all that I desired, why would I self-destruct?" The answer is simple ... because you were not ready to deal with the other side of the rainbow.

As a karma buster, I want to prepare you for all aspects of this journey. Many believe major breakthroughs are the keys to success, and, to a large degree, that is true. You must also be prepared to deal with and adjust to your newfound success.

I have known a number of people who were very successful on Wall Street. This led many of them down a path of self-destruction and over-indulgence. As I said earlier, the negative ego is just sitting there waiting for you to lose yourself in the process.

How to Avoid the Pitfalls of the Other Side

The work I have done on myself has always been dedicated to moving forward and not losing my spiritual connection. Working spiritually forces you to have the ultimate respect for the power of the negative ego. You have to love and honor yourself without becoming full of yourself. This is not as easy as you may imagine.

As you become more powerful, it is very easy to start judging and feeling superior. Don't go there. Keep your ego in check and know that you are not better or worse than anyone else. Your awareness can take you out this place of high ego very quickly. Give yourself a break. You are only human and still susceptible to the trappings of the flesh.

Dealing with future feelings will help you as you make your transition. Anticipating these feelings will put you in a much better position as things begin to change. This is like preparing for a marathon. Runners will tell you they build up their distance over time, but they never run the full 26.2 miles before the race. They leave a little piece of the unknown to enhance the experience. They are ready ... but now they will have to cross a threshold they have never experienced along the way.

Entrepreneurs, for example, are very focused on what they want to accomplish. This amazing focus helps them stay on track regardless of what is happening around them. It is a sort of tunnel vision. Creative types and inventors often share this focus. All of their energy is focused on the end result, the prize. Then, after years of hard work and dedication, they succeed.

Yet when many of them look back, they see a path of personal destruction, complete with broken families, destroyed friendships, health issues and, in many cases, bitter feelings.

Was it worth it? Do I need this level of focus and dedication to be successful? Yes ... but at what cost?

The key is dealing with your feelings along the way. It is not possible to maintain perfect balance, but you must try. Blind focus moves you into a lower state of awareness and disconnects you from spirit. Many successful, happy people have been able to maintain balance and not lose themselves in the process. They were ready for the other side of the rainbow. You will be too.

You are going to prepare yourself by acknowledging that there is another side. Most people are focused only on the prize, winning and nothing else. They are not aware of potential dangers that are waiting for them. You, my friend, will be ready and prepared to deal with the other side.

The logical question is what could possibly be negative about getting everything we want in life? It seems absurd in the realm of what seems to make sense, but we are not playing in the world of logic. This is the world of feelings, emotions and desires. Throw logic out the window.

So you want to be...

- a huge success in business.
- rich and famous.
- fit and sexy.
- healthy and vital.
- in a loving relationship.

Who doesn't?

Now you have to move into the feelings associated with your desires. How will it feel to be rich and famous? At first blush, it seems like the greatest thing in the world. You have money, people love you, your work is admired, you are in demand. What is the other side of this situation? You have money and people will want you to take care of them. You are criticized more often. People think your work stinks. Your time is being pressed, as more people desire your services or ask for favors.

As you can see, there are many other feelings to deal with on the other side of the rainbow. There may be more pressure and stress dealing with your newfound success than you originally imagined. You may feel guilty because you can't help every person who seeks your assistance.

How do you prepare for this?

You feel the feelings before you arrive.

I was working with an up and coming actor in Los Angeles. We were working on his breaking through and becoming a star. First, we worked on his karma, which brought him back to some issues with his mom. Then we moved into the feelings of being famous. He was shocked when a feeling of complete terror swept through his body. "I can't believe this. I feel like I am so over my head," he cried. There was complete panic and fear on the other side.

Now we can be logical. I know you thinking people will like this part. Doesn't it make perfect sense to avoid something that is going to move you into a feeling of panic? This fear was holding him back. Moving forward required this young star to face the feelings waiting for him on the other side of the rainbow.

Your journey will be exactly the same. There will be feelings of great discomfort and stress on the other side. Begin by imagining yourself in the situation you seek and then move into your feelings.

How will you feel when you are:

- in great shape?
- in a loving relationship?
- successful in your career?
- doing the work you love?

I used to do this when I wanted to imagine myself speaking in front of huge audiences. In the beginning, I was overwhelmed with terror and felt I was not good enough for this type of event. The more you identify and feel these feelings, the easier your transition will be.

It is virtually impossible to know and feel all potential feelings, but you can make significant progress just by doing this exercise. Keep asking yourself "how will I feel when I arrive at my destination?" Then move into the feeling and allow yourself to feel it on a deep emotional level.

You are creating something foreign and new. It takes time to make your positive creation normal in your life. We have all been creating pain for so long, it seems unnatural to create what we desire. Be patient. In time you will create the life you love with ease – and you will feel great about it.

10 Allowing Yourself to Receive

Most people believe they are not receiving what they desire when in reality they are not *allowing* it to come to them. This is a major shift in thinking and awareness. We are conditioned to be great givers and terrible receivers. One of the oldest sayings in our culture is "It is better to give than to receive." Why is it better and not just as good?

I have worked with many powerful teachers along my journey. When something good happened to me, each would say, "How nice it is that you *allowed* that to come into your life right now." No one ever talked about what I had done to make it happen. We always discussed how I allowed it to happen.

This concept was beyond foreign to me. The more I heard the word 'allow,' the more it resonated in my soul. Over time, this concept began to make more sense. It took many years before I truly accepted it on a deeper emotional level. Overcoming a life-time of beliefs is not easy.

The principle of allowance offers a whole new way of interacting with the world. As you move through your negative energy and begin to let go, you begin to realize all you have to do is step aside and allow the universe to show you the way.

I had a very powerful experience with the principle of allowance in my last job in the corporate world. At the time, I was not aware of the magnitude of this experience. I had been working in corporate America for more than eight years. During this time, I had received a few promotions and moved up to better jobs. But I was unable to break through to the better management positions with the higher salaries I desired.

After a few years, I became frustrated. It was time to start searching for a new job. I was looking within my current company for a better opportunity, with the encouragement of my boss. In addition, I was seeking employment outside the company. I remember feeling upset about my current position and level of compensation. This was a feeling I had not experienced before with this type of intensity.

A few months passed and there was absolutely no opportunity on the horizon. Finally, I decided to stop looking and accept my situation. Maybe the universe wanted me to stay where I was and work on my current business. I had started to develop my training program on a part-time basis a few years earlier. My ultimate goal was to leave the corporate world and do my training work full-time. After all, this was a job I could do in my sleep and the salary was decent. I allowed myself to let go and stop chasing a new job.

A few weeks later, I received a phone call from an employment agency I had contacted four years earlier. I had never heard back from this agency after speaking to a representative and submitting my information. The woman on the phone now told me there was a company interested in speaking to me about a National Sales Director position. She told me the company was based in London and the executives were coming to New York City to conduct a series of interviews. I agreed to meet with them on a hot day in August. As I walked toward the meeting, I realized I had absolutely no expectations.

We had a great session and I was called back for a second interview. Within four weeks I had accepted the new position, doubled my current salary and found myself sitting on a plane headed to London for training. As I sat in my business class seat on Virgin Atlantic Airlines, I remember thinking 'how did this all happen?' It was so simple, smooth and fast. I was amazed at how easy it all seemed to be.

I had spent months sending out resumés, going on interviews and negotiating with potential employers. I was chasing down leads and frantically trying to make something happen. Then I stopped and everything happened … like magic.

Without knowing it, I had stumbled upon a very powerful principle. It took me years to fully understand and appreciate this experience. I had discovered "The Principle of Allowance."

This was exactly the type of position I was seeking. I had been focusing on an executive position with a higher salary and an employment contract. I was desperately chasing this position without success. The minute I relaxed and let go of the tension, the job magically appeared. The amazing thing was that it happened so quickly. Had you laid out this scenario to me six weeks earlier, I would have thought you were insane. In a few weeks my life changed completely.

By letting go, I had cleared the path for the universe to deliver. As I remembered back, I realized I was in the same state when I met my wife. I had had a series of bad relationships and was resigned to being a bachelor. A few months later, I met my amazing wife of over twenty years.

This memory prompted me to go back and look at all of the good things in my life. I call it my *Serendipity List.* I went back to my childhood and made a list of all the wonderful experiences and people who had entered my life. As I did this, I realized all of the wonderful people I met and the great events I experienced just seemed to happen. They were not the result of some grand plan or brilliant idea. It was also clear to me that I was not chasing these things. I desired something, let go and waited to receive it.

There was no feeling of pressure or distress. I simply focused and let the desire go. There was no obsessive thinking or extreme planning. I held my focus and was in a state of total relaxation.

Allowance only happens when you let go. You cannot force things to happen as your negative ego desires. They must occur in a natural, organic manner. You must be able to let go and trust for the universe to deliver. You must surrender and trust that all things will come to you when you are ready to receive them.

One Key Difference This Time

Like most people, I had, and have, many desires. Many times these desires never came to fruition. Some were minor, while others, like my job search, were major. In this magical job search case, something very different had actually happened. In the past, I wanted a better job with a higher salary. This time around, I truly believed I deserved it. There is a huge gap between desire and belief.

Although I had desires in the past, I did not have the deep feeling I truly deserved them. After eight years of sitting in corporate meetings and taking direction from guys in suits, I realized something very important – these guys were no better than me. I had always believed all of these people in corner offices truly were better. I finally felt and believed there was no difference. I deserved the same money and respect as they did.

As this feeling first washed over me, I began to feel angry. This was not ordinary anger on a surface level. It was much deeper and filled with intense emotion. I knew I was worth more and I was sure I deserved it. I held this feeling even after giving up the job search. My anger slowly turned to inner confidence and a strong feeling of deserving. I was now ready to receive what I desired.

That was the moment when my inner desires became aligned with my sense of true worth. The minute this happened, it triggered the "Principle of Allowance." Now I was ready, I believed and I allowed it to happen. It all began with a sense of knowing I had value. I did not just know it … I felt it deep in my heart and soul. I held onto that feeling and the universe did the rest.

You must feel you deserve what you desire on a very deep emotional level. When these elements align, you are open to receive anything you desire. Manifesting your desires requires you to truly feel you deserve them. You must then hold this energy to create the desired outcome. You can want something all day long. Until you truly feel you are worthy, it will not come to you.

Steps to Help You Allow

Although this is an organic process, I realize that in the third dimensional world we like to have specific steps to follow. Below you will see an outlined plan that will help you allow your desires to come to fruition. Follow the steps, but understand this is not a linear process. Be flexible and understand there are no set timelines.

Step 1: Know Your True Desire

Your true desires come from deep inside your soul. They are coded to your DNA and aligned with your mission here on earth. They are the burning feelings, the passions, you are carrying and they have nothing to do with what your family wants.

These are the feelings that wake you up at night – the powerful desires motivating you. What do you want in your life? Know it and own it, or stay stuck in a world of mediocrity. You may not have an exact picture of your desires at this time. It does not matter. All of the details will become clear as you move forward.

I started my career as a sales and marketing trainer. My desire was to help others through teaching. I was interested in personal development and always added an element of it to all of my classes. At no time did I ever imagine doing this type of work. Becoming a spiritual energy teacher and healer was not on my radar screen when I started.

I was on the right path, and allowed the universe to guide me forward. Stay focused on your desires. Do not be concerned if you are not completely clear about your desires. Take a step forward and let go.

Step 2: Feel You Truly Deserve It

This is a tricky piece of the process because you are convinced you deserve it mentally, on a conscious level. If you are not creating what you desire (the process doesn't seem to be working for you), there might be a gap. Your feelings are the key to opening the doors of allowance. You must search your feelings and be in truth. I was frustrated for years in the corporate world, always thinking I was worth more. As I moved deeper into my feelings, however, I realized I did not believe I deserved more money and a better position. I did not really feel worthy of it.

This is a very difficult truth to accept, but it is critical. Be honest and look at how you really feel. Do you believe you are worthy? Go deeper and deeper until you uncover your truth. This is a process and it will take some time. When you feel that surge and a peak of anger, you are on your way. The anger will pass quickly. All it is really doing is bringing your true feelings to the surface.

Your feelings are the driving force of your energy. The key is to be brutally honest with how you feel about yourself. This honesty will unlock the door to your truth and help you move forward. Accepting your truth will release energy and open the door to new opportunities.

Once I accepted my truth of not feeling worthy at that time, I was free. The resistance and pressure were removed and I was able to get into my true feelings.

Step 3: Hold Your Focus with Emotion

One of the big issues we face as human beings is the ability to hold our focus. You must hold your energy long enough to create what you desire. Energy works on the premises of focus and expansion. Whatever you focus on most will hold the highest level of power. When you hold energy with emotion, you are creating a powerful force that will not be denied.

The universe is non-judgmental. This is not about you being good or bad. It is a simple matter of holding your focus with emotion. If you hold negative feelings on an emotional level, you are sure to create a negative outcome. The scenario I described about my new job was a product of this principle. I truly felt I deserved a better position with a much higher salary. That feeling never left, even after I decided to stop looking for a new job. I was still holding the belief, focus and emotion regarding my value.

Decide on exactly what you desire. Tap into the feelings and emotions connected to your desire. Continue to hold that focus and feeling every day. Do not worry about how or when it will happen. Start each day by focusing on your desire and feeling the emotion connected to it.

Step 4: Surrender and Trust

Here comes the hardest part. You are focused and excited about your new desire. In the process you start to feel you truly deserve it on a deep emotional level. I remember when I decided I wanted to do my training work in 1991. It was very exciting and then reality hit me … now what? How will I do this?

Let go of your desire to control the situation and the exact outcome. Surrender and know that the universe is already helping you. You may not see it right away, but believe me, it is happening. Energy is always in motion. You may not see things changing. Not to worry. Your energy is already moving your desires closer to you. Trust that you will receive exactly what you desire when the time is right.

Occasionally you will become frustrated and impatient. That happens to us all every now and then. Shake it off and go back to your focus. If all of your desires were delivered immediately, there would be no challenge. Here in the third dimensional world, we live for challenge. Embrace your desire and relax. It is on the way to you right now.

Step 5: Deal with Your Feelings

Along the journey, you will encounter many feelings. These feelings must be addressed and cleared if you are to move forward. Use the meditations outlined earlier on a regular basis to stay connected to how you feel.

Any time you repress or ignore a strong feeling, you will remain stuck. Resist the desire to act out or move into repression. The more you feel, the easier this process will be for you.

Step 6: Follow Your Guides

We all have guides on the other side who are attempting to help us every day. The problem is that most of us are so trapped in our negative egos, we are unable to pick up these signals. As our energy flow opens, we will see these signs more clearly. Some will be obvious, while others may be quite subtle. The higher your energy vibration, the easier it will be to identify these signs and validations.

Guides communicate in many ways. It may be a song on the radio, a thought to call someone, an invitation to attend an event or a new idea. Start to ask your guides for help and validations. They are waiting to hear from you.

A few years ago I was working on a new idea for a book called "Spiritual Selling." When I have a new idea, I immediately buy the domain name online. The name spiritualselling.com was already taken. I remember thinking "this may not be the direction to go in right now." During my daily meditations I started to ask my guides, "What is the best direction for me now?" I would ask for a sign every day.

Approximately three weeks later, I received an email from a man I had coached a few years earlier. He was a technical guy who was going through a difficult time and was in the middle of a divorce. His finances were in shambles as a result. I told him the coaching was on me and not to worry about it. I had not heard from him in almost two years.

His email said, "Hey, Joe. I see you are working on some cool stuff. I saw your new idea for spiritual selling. One night I was playing around online and I saw spiritualselling.com was available. I bought it for you."

A few months later I made a deal with a publisher to distribute "Spiritual Selling."

This was an amazing piece of guidance and validation. As I said, your guides are always ready to help you. All you have to do is ask. Some of your messages will be bolts of lightning, like my book name spiritualselling.com story. Others will be subtle and will require a little more attention to detail. In time you will see these messages very clearly. They are always there for you to use along your journey.

Step 7: Allow Your Desire to Enter

Many people follow the first six steps, only to fall short just as their desire is about to manifest. You may find that hard to believe, but I see this happen every day. There are always feelings of fear when you are about to receive something you have desired for so long. The change requires that you let go of your old identity. For many people this is too much change to accept, so they opt to remain stuck in their old energy.

Imagine yourself standing in front of a series of doors. Behind each door is an amazing gift just waiting for you. All you have to do is open the door and step through to receive your wondrous gift ... your dream business or career, your soul mate, great health or incredible wealth, to name a few. You are standing there, knowing exactly what is on the other side of the door and ... you refuse to open it!

"*Crazy,*" you say? There are millions of people who refuse to step through one of these doors every minute of every day.

Why? Because you have to let of go of the old you and become reborn.

Jane Refused to Enter

A woman we knew, let's call her Jane, was constantly complaining about her job in a local retail store. She was always talking about working for a larger chain with health benefits and a 401K plan. Jane was very emotional about her situation and held this negative energy for a number of years. One day, a friend introduced her to the manager of a large retail chain. Jane was interviewed and offered a job.

Perfect ... right? But no, Jane turned down the offer and went back to the small retail store, and continued to complain. Jane did not want to give that up.

Jane followed the first six steps I outlined exactly. She had a clear desire, felt she deserved it, held her focus, surrendered and accepted where she was at the time, felt her feelings and followed her guides. This led to an interview for the perfect job she desired. Jane had allowed all of these things to unfold in her life. So why didn't Jane allow herself to accept the job she truly desired?

This is, of course, a very big question because it makes absolutely no sense. Why would someone come so far and then walk away from desire at the last minute? There are many reasons, all based on the feelings and beliefs I have been discussing. When you stop yourself from attaining your desire in a situation like this, there are three key feelings holding you back.

Those feelings are … ***Fear, Guilt and Unworthiness.*** You may face any one or all three of these deep feelings.

Jane was unable to step through the door because it meant she had to let go of her old identity. She had to give up being a victim and complaining. Jane is addicted to these feelings and refuses to give them up. I know this may seem inconceivable but it happens all the time. People do not like giving up the negative ego identity that has become so comfortable. They fear moving into a new world, even though they know it will be better on a conscious level.

When you find yourself stuck, look to one of these feelings – ***Fear, Guilt and Unworthiness.***

Why You Won't Allow Yourself to Receive

On a conscious level none of this makes sense, yet it happens every day. We see celebrities, athletes, politicians and wealthy business people, all having seemingly everything, screw up their lives regularly. Primarily this is based on feelings of discomfort and conflict.

Why you are unable to receive (all based on your feelings and beliefs):

- You do not feel worthy
- You feel guilt when you receive
- You are fearful you cannot deliver (feelings of incompetency)

- There is too much pressure to remain in a higher position (more money, better health, more responsibility, more demands on your time)
- You cannot receive positive attention or compliments
- You refuse to give up your old identity (you like pain too much)
- You have a great fear of the unknown
- You are conditioned to give and never receive
- You are addicted to feeling bad about yourself and complaining
- There is a deep conflict between your beliefs and desires ("I am not supposed to have all of these wonderful people and opportunities in my life")
- You feel tremendous discomfort

Any time you feel stuck, refer to this list. One or more of these feelings will be at the core of your inability to allow something wonderful to come onto your life. As you accept and address these feelings, the block will be removed. Then you will allow yourself to receive what you desire. Releasing negative energy requires you to feel your feelings and emotions. The third dimensional world is filled with ups and downs. Regardless of how great you may be doing now, eventually you will have to deal with another difficult feeling. The difference is that now you will have the tools to move forward quickly.

When you cross over and move your energy to a higher level, there will always be intense feelings of discomfort. It is important to expect these feelings before they arrive. When you know these feelings are coming, it becomes much easier to deal with them. When you go from struggle to success, there is a major shift of energy. It takes a while to reach a level of comfort in your new position.

Follow these 7 steps to unlock your power of allowance ...

Step 1: Know Your True Desire

Step 2: Feel You Truly Deserve It

Step 3: Hold Your Focus with Emotion

Step 4: Surrender and Trust

Step 5: Deal with Your Feelings

Step 6: Follow Your Guides

Step 7: Allow Your Desire to Enter

In the world of energy the principle of allowance is easy and flowing. Here on earth we must first overcome ourselves to unlock this power. The desire to control and manipulate is very powerful for many of us. Moving away from logic and moving into your feelings is the key to this transition. Be patient as you move from the dense world of over-thinking to the world of feelings and flow.

Stop Chasing Success and Happiness

Imagine yourself as a child running and playing. You woke up every morning with a sense of wonder and excitement. Anything seemed possible and the day revolved around fun. There was no need for too much thinking or planning in those days. You were not concerned with business plans, contracts, credit cards or complicated investments. You just wanted to have fun. You allowed yourself to run free and enjoy life.

What happened?

When did all of this freedom and wonder leave you?

Why did you stop allowing yourself to have fun?

It all started going downhill when you realized there were responsibilities in life. You began to over-think. All of a sudden, you had to have a plan for your future. There were grades, jobs, bills, money, relationships and many other burdens to deal with. Your focus quickly shifted from fun to responsibility.

We seem to lose our full sense of wonder at some point. There are special people who seem to hold on to their youthful spirit. These people are truly blessed. Many others show no signs of the carefree child who once inhabited their adult body. How and when did you lose this wonderful kid? It happens for many reasons and at different times based on your background and family. We are all trying to find our way back to the *Yellow Brick Road.*

The real trouble started when you were told you had to do something to get something. This turned you into a chaser instead of a receiver. Chasers are constantly trying to catch the elusive dream. Just when you believe you have caught this dream, it slips through your fingers like grains of sand. Yet you continue to chase the elusive prize. You have been conditioned to believe that all dreams can come true only if you willing to work hard enough and keep chasing them.

I know a lot of poor people who work very hard. Why aren't they getting their piece of the pie?

Once you begin to chase, you are blocking energy. When this happens, you stop allowing the universe to deliver your desires. You now believe you must go out and chase to receive what you want.

Why would you want to chase something when all you have to do is sit back and let the universe deliver the goods? You chase because you have been conditioned to believe you must. You cannot dictate when these deliveries will arrive, and you want them now, so you would rather chase them in a desperate attempt to control than allow them to flow.

Allowing requires you to give up the desire to control and manipulate. Now you have to learn to sit back and receive. I know what you are thinking, "*Joe, this sounds great…when do I start?*" You may start at any time. As you will see, making this shift in your belief system and feelings will be more challenging than you can ever imagine.

Chasing is also part of your karma. Look at your parents and identify what they were chasing. Were they chasing approval, attention, accolades, respect, understanding or just plain old love?

My father was the youngest of 12. His mother did not give him the attention he was seeking. My aunts would always tell me how they raised him and took care of him. Their mother was older and did not give him the love and attention he desired. As a result, he spent his life chasing attention. He believed that becoming known for something would finally bring her attention to him.

It started with baseball. My dad was a top prospect in high school and was drafted by the New York Giants, now the San Francisco Giants. He believed becoming a baseball player would attract the attention he desired. After an injury, his career was cut short. He then moved into the New York City Police Department and eventually became a narcotics detective. Some of his friends received acclaim for major cases they broke. Two of his former partners even became famous, then had a book and movie made about their big case called *The French Connection.*

He dreamed of one day cracking a big case of his own. My dad chased this objective with intense ferocity. As a result, he became disconnected from his family and lost himself in the process. This course of action led him into dangerous situations and ultimately to his death.

Working through my karma I saw myself doing the same thing with my work. I had an obsession with bringing this work to the world – at all costs. Once I saw the similarity to my father, I realized this was not the road I wanted to travel. It was important to let go of my obsessive feelings and just do the work I was meant to do. I had to stop chasing. This was the karma my father passed on to me. If I continued on my path, it would have led to destruction and even death.

You will see some of this in yourself as you become more aware. What are you chasing and why? Ask yourself these questions when you notice a feeling of pressure or when you disconnect from source. It will help you get back on track and reconnect to spirit.

Busting your karma moves you into receiving mode. You realize that you are supposed to be receiving and it is meant to be easy. We are conditioned to believe it is hard but that is just the nature of conditioning. The universe wants you to be happy and in a state of flow.

Our experience here is about reconnecting to our true spirit. The journey is the fun part, believe it or not. Now I can look back and appreciate all of my challenges. The struggles and surges of emotion were, and will continue to be, the most exciting part of my experience. As you continue your journey, you will appreciate the work you have done and the experiences you have been blessed to feel.

Daily Joy

You may have heard the expression *What would Jesus do?* This is designed to help people think about their actions before they do something hurtful. In our house we say "*What would Eric do?*" Eric is our son and he brings great joy to our lives. He is the master of creating happiness.

Even now, as he is getting ready to enter college, he still holds this energy. He is constantly seeking joy and fun in his life. As we become adults, we lose this feeling. How many days do you wake up in the morning and ask yourself what joyful thing will I do today?

I know you are busy and have responsibilities, but can't you squeeze a little joy somewhere into each day? Maybe it's a cup of that special coffee, reading a new book, listening to music or a walk in the park after work. It does not have to be anything dramatic. Just a little dose of daily joy goes a long way.

Every day your assignment is to make sure you do at least one thing that brings you joy. I always look to Eric when I am losing that feeling of joy. He is the master of keeping joy in his day.

So I ask you ...*What would Eric do?*

11 Turning on the Lights

Busting your karma is about moving into the light. You are becoming enlightened as you let go of the old and elevate your energy vibration. Now you are creating the life you came here to live.

You are able to see things you were blind to in the past. At your new level of clarity, you see the entire world in a whole new way. The funny thing is that this wisdom was always around you. In your old energy and negative karma, you were unable to see it.

This thought reminded me of a time when I was shopping for sunglasses. I was walking through a mall and came upon a kiosk selling sunglasses. We were getting ready to take a driving trip and I needed a new pair for the road. The woman at the kiosk showed me a few different styles and asked, "Will you be using these glasses for driving?" I told her I was and she suggested the polarized glasses designed to protect your eyes from the sun and reduce eye strain.

I was curious as to what made polarized glasses different.

She said, "Put on this pair and look at the frame." There was a blank white sheet of paper in a wooden frame. "What do you see?" she queried.

"Nothing. It is a blank white page in a frame," I replied.

She handed me the polarized pair and asked me to look at the same frame. This time I saw a dragon where there was nothing before. The dragon was always there but I needed the right glasses to see it.

This is exactly what happens when we step into the light and elevate our awareness. Now you can see life in an entirely new way. You will also see others in a whole new way as you begin to live an enlightened life.

There are many stages of enlightenment. Every time you experience a new realization or a deep truth is uncovered you are in the light. As you shed the old karma you will spend a lot more time in this place of higher knowledge and clarity.

Once you know and see these truths, there is no turning back. Now that you know, you cannot unknow. This is a blessing but it can also be a curse if you are not in full acceptance at all times. You will see many people who are not living in the light and may feel compelled to judge them. This will block your energy and flow.

Another common occurrence is the desire to share what you have learned to help others. It is natural and exciting to feel the desire to share these principles with people you see suffering. Many of these people will want nothing to do with you or your story of karma busting. Do not take this personally. These people are not ready for the work at this time. I spent many years in a state of frustration trying to help people who did not want to be helped. On one level it made me feel I was doing a bad job trying to explain what I had discovered. Now I know it had nothing to do with me. Each person's journey is unique to them.

Allow them to have their experience without judgment.

Now I see myself as a fisherman. All I have to do is place my line in the water. You may choose to jump on or swim past the message. In the end, it is all perfect … the world, corruption, greed, violence, suffering, even reality television. You must see it this way because it helps you remove the judgment.

We can also choose to experience the love and joy in every moment.

On earth we require both sides of the emotional spectrum to have a meaningful experience. Know that everything coming into your consciousness is meant to be there. Accept everything and look for the messages you are receiving. Being more aware will accelerate your process and move you through the negative karma much faster.

Living in the light is very different. More and more people are living this life every day. As you elevate your energy and awareness, you will attract more people of like mind and spirit. This will happen organically so there is no need to push it. All you have to do is allow yourself to receive.

As you move through your karma and get off your Karmic Wheel, you will no longer be creating your life based on the past. The events and feelings of your old life will no longer serve you. There are many aspects, layers and pieces to your karma.

You will clear energy in one area and immediately move on to the next one. The difference is now you have the tools to identify and then clear the old energy and move forward. Accept this power and remain humble. Resist the negative ego's desire to bring you down.

If you are a Spiderman fan, you will know this famous line, "With great power comes great responsibility." Accept your new power and use it wisely. Express no judgment or negative feelings towards others.

Love everyone even though you may not like them. Love yourself all day long and know the world is perfect – and so are you!

Also by Joe Nunziata

Books

Spiritual Selling

Finding Your Purpose

No More 9 to 5

Home Study Programs

Spiritual Selling

No More Mental Barriers

No More 9 to 5

Audio Programs

Change Your Energy, Change Your Life

Membership Program
Ultra Breakthrough Club

Receive enlightening and inspirational new training sessions each month.

See details and try now at:
www.ultrabreakthrough.com

See more at www.JoeNunz.com

CPSIA information can be obtained at www.ICGtesting.com
Printed in the USA
LVOW060318190312

273654LV00001B/4/P